The Embarrassed Believer

Reviving Christian Witness
in an Age of Unbelief

HUGH HEWITT

WORD PUBLISHING
Nashville·London·Vancouver·Melbourne

THE EMBARRASSED BELIEVER

Unless otherwise indicated, Scripture quotations used in this book are from the Revised Standard Version of the Bible. Copyright © 1946, 1952, 1971, 1973 by the Division of Christian Education of the National Council of the Churches of Christ in the USA. Used by permission.

Other scriptures come from the following sources:

The King James Version of the Bible (KJV).

The New King James Version (NKJV), copyright © 1979, 1980, 1982, 1992, Thomas Nelson, Inc., Publisher.

The Holy Bible, New International Version. Copyright © 1973, 1978, 1984 by International Bible Society. Used by permission of Zondervan Publishing House. All rights reserved. The "NIV" and "New International Version" trademarks are registered in the United States Patent and Trademark Office by International Bible Society. Use of either trademark requires the permission of International Bible Society.

The New Revised Standard Version of the Bible, copyright © 1989 by the Division of Christian Education of the National Council of the Churches of Christ in the United States of America. Used by permission.

Published in association with Sealy M. Yates, Literary Agent, Orange, California.

Library of Congress Cataloging-in-Publication Data

Hewitt, Hugh, 1956—
   The embarrassed believer : reviving Christian witness in an age of unbelief
Hugh Hewitt.
     p. cm.
   ISBN 0-8499-1419-1
    1. Witness bearing (Christianity) 2. Evangelistic work. 3. Apologetics.
4. Civilization, Modern—1950- I. Title.
BV4520.H48   1998
239—dc21   98-12105
                                           CIP

  ISBN 0-8499-1485-X (hardcover)

Printed in the United States of America.
9 0 1 2 3 4 5 9 BVG 9 8 7 6 5 4 3 2 1

First Hardcover Edition for Christian Family Book Club: 1999

For
Marg and Bill Hewitt

Contents

Introduction: Perfect Pitch

I n the past two years, I've interviewed four authors who among themselves have sold more than ten million books.

Robert Fulghum is the author of *All I Really Need to Know I Learned in Kindergarten* and a half-dozen other titles. A Unitarian minister and a music teacher, Fulghum was "discovered" when a copy of some of his writings made it into the right publisher's hands.

James Redfield authored *The Celestine Prophecy* and its sequel, *The Tenth Insight*. Redfield could not interest a publisher in his first book, so he published and marketed it himself. It took off. And off. And off.

Robert Bly was already an accomplished poet when he published *Iron John* and launched the "men's movement." Though that movement has subsequently been much mocked, it proved a powerful trigger for some men. Even a Christian skeptical of Bly's fuzzy theology would have to credit some of the success of Promise Keepers to the path blazed by Bly and his companions.

Marianne Williamson wrote *A Return to Love* as a follow-up to her wildly popular taped commentaries on *The Book of Miracles*. Williamson is a favorite of Oprah's, and even her most recent offering, *The Healing of America,* was heavily plugged on that show, though it is a political as opposed to "spiritual" book.

All four of these authors were promoting books when they came through Los Angeles. Fulghum had just issued *True Love,* a collection of stories about various affairs of the heart. It is a series of endearing vignettes of no substantial weight, but very pleasant. Fulghum himself is a perfect gentleman, a man to whom fame has happened but upon whom fame has left no serious scars. He and his charming wife greeted me and the crew in a swank hotel and gave us as much time as was needed to produce a tight ten minutes of tape, but we might as well have been having coffee in any Starbucks. In other words, Fulghum is as pleasant and unassuming a hyper-best-selling author as you can imagine.

The other three came to the KCET studios in East Hollywood, where *Life & Times,* the show I have co-hosted for five years, is produced for daily airing throughout central and southern California. Once a week we broadcast throughout the entire state. KCET is the Los Angeles affiliate of PBS, and my show, which airs after the *Newshour with Jim Lehrer,* is a highly prized promotional stop for most authors. It's PBS. It's prime time. And the hosts actually read the books.

Authors with books that fall into the category of "moral cartography" are generally served up to me. These are my favorite interviews. Whether it's Greg Laurie, the young pastor who launched the Harvest Crusades, or Cardinal Roger Mahoney, a prince of the Roman Catholic Church, or theological renegade Robert Funk, whose Jesus Seminar has seduced the media elite, or Talmud giant Adin Steinsaltz, or Kaballah teacher David Aaron, or even '60s-radical-turned-politician-turned-eclectic-mystic Tom Hayden, I get 'em all. My seat is not limited to the cosmic-picture players. I'm a sucker for fame as well—Oliver Stone, Charlton Heston, Richard Dreyfuss, all were great fun to interview at length. But I have displayed an enthusiasm for discussing the "ultimate issues" that the show's producers have been kind enough to honor as best they can.

The four authors I mentioned earlier—Bly, Redfield, Fulghum, and Williamson—have sold millions and millions of books. They are very nice people. Each is witty and possesses a certain charisma. Bly's the old wizard, dispensing his version of the great, enduring truths. Fulghum's Santa Claus—he looks it—with a bag not of toys but aphorisms. Redfield and Williamson are the superstars of New Age chic.

But, sad to say, hardly one word that any of these folks wrote is of lasting value. I genuinely doubt that any one of their books has more than a single generation's worth of shelf life. They are authors who represent a particular age and mind-set. Because they have perfect pitch for these times, they cannot print their books fast enough.

(And when they depart from the formula, as Bly did with the *The Sibling Society,* their sales plummet.) But when the music changes—and it will change, for it always does—their books will drop from sight.

Their individual and collective success raises some important questions. What is that perfect pitch? What song is this quartet of sirens singing?

Very simple: Meaning.

Meaning without sharp edges. Meaning without giving offense. It is no accident that the best-selling book invented for script purposes in the summer 1997 blockbuster movie *Contact* had *The Search for Meaning* as its title. The four authors I interviewed know this hunger for meaning, and they have invented various theories of how to infuse it into life in the '90s. These men and woman are the heralds of an "everyone's OK" theology. And they sell millions of books because we all need a theology and we have beaten down believers who hold truths that offend. When orthodoxy collapsed under numerous assaults, the need for truth and order did not dissolve. Into that vacuum where once orthodox Christianity supplied answers flooded the self and the theology of self.

There is an unkind thing to be said that I regret having to say: *The Celestine Prophecy* is a wretched book. I have yet to meet a reader of good books who thought it well written. It was a chore to finish, and *The Tenth Insight* was worse. But this pair of books has sold and sold and sold. And the devoted legions of Redfield fans can certainly dismiss my criticism with the accurate observation that this little book now in your hands is no threat to match the circulation of Mr. Redfield's newsletter, much less his books.

I point out the quality of Redfield's effort only to contrast it with the awesome nature of his success. If the product is so poor—you read it, you decide—what powers the phenomenon of its sales? Obviously a need for meaning is being met. What's the need? How's it being met?

Christians know the joy and the comfort of Christ. Some can articulate these things with great passion, precision, and eloquence. Others are tongue-tied but no less satisfied.

The folks buying Redfield—and especially those recommending

him to others—cannot be Christians, for Christians know his beliefs are hokum. The same conclusion holds for Fulghum, Bly, and Williamson, though their respective arguments with orthodoxy are more muted than Redfield's. Christians of a genuine sort are not fans of these folks. And—the key point—they cannot be. Genuine Christianity must absolutely reject these offerings as hokum. No need for book burnings, of course, but there is a clear need to label nonsense as nonsense.

I once heard a fine theologian, Ray Ortlund Jr., preach a sermon on the difference between authentic and nominal Christians. Authentic Christians had "closed with Christ," he argued. They knew the significance of the cross; they "got it."

Nominal Christians, on the other hand, did not.

I suspect nominal Christians by the thousands, if not millions, have bought and enjoyed one or more of these four authors and their books. Because they have not "closed with Christ," they do not recoil from the fractured heresies of these authors.

Which, finally, brings me to this book.

Where has the gospel gone, that so much space—such vast space—is left for these slanders upon salvation?

For that is what these bestsellers are: slanders on the atoning crucifixion and resurrection of Christ, a crucifixion and resurrection that for twenty centuries have guided the central nervous system of the Western mind.

If the Christian story is true, how did it come to pass that these books have not only succeeded but have dwarfed the success of even the most successful orthodox American writers? If the Christian story is true, in the sense that the statement that water freezes at thirty-two degrees is true, then all of these books could not succeed in a market powered by genuine Christians. But they *have* succeeded. Why?

The answer is, I think, fairly straightforward: The Embarrassed Believer. Consider this statement:

"Whoever is ashamed of me and of my words in this adulterous and sinful generation, of him will the Son of man also be ashamed, when he comes in the glory of his Father's with the holy angels" (Mark 8:38). That's Jesus Christ talking. He is direct. He is speaking

to the Embarrassed Believer, cowed and hiding at the end of the millennium.

"I am not ashamed of the gospel," wrote Paul to the Romans. "It
is the power of God for salvation to every one who has faith, to the
Jew first and also to the Greek" (Romans 1:16). When Paul penned
that bold proclamation, he was preaching to a world more than
merely hostile to his faith. It was a world willing to execute believers.
In other words, there was in Paul's day a very genuine risk to belief.

Yet the imprisoned Paul wrote to his colleague Timothy, "Do not
be ashamed then of testifying to our Lord, nor of me his prisoner."
Time and the authorities had caught up with Paul. Tradition holds
that he was executed in Rome around the year A.D. 60. When he
wrote to Timothy it is almost certain that he knew the price he
would eventually pay. Still, he urged Timothy to "share in suffering
for the gospel in the power of God, who saved us and called us with
a holy calling, not in virtue of our works but in virtue of his own
purpose and the grace which he gave us in Christ Jesus ages ago"
(2 Timothy 1:8–9).

Now the Embarrassed Believer has already begun to put some distance between Christ's words cited above and herself, between Paul's
double imperative and himself. The Embarrassed Believer is happy
to have nearly two thousand years of possible ambiguity to put
between Scripture and today. Boldness and embarrassment mean
different things in different centuries, right?

On February 12, 1997, a dozen Egyptian Christians were gunned
down by terrorists in a city just a two-hour drive from Cairo.
Another thirteen were murdered a month later in a different city.
Egyptian Christians practice their faith with a real sense of peril at
their elbows.

From Paul's imprisonment and martyrdom through to this year's
murders of Christians around the globe, there is an ennobling and
inspiring thread of courage uniting saint after saint. It is an inheritance of every believer.

The power of this inheritance to inspire boldness varies dramati-
cally, however, and nowhere does the church appear less confident
than in the United States. Certainly there are vigorous congregations and passionate preachers. There are new movements, new

leaders, and new means and methods of evangelism. But there is also a far more pervasive self-censorship and timidity among even the most devoted and authentic Christians.

This is a book for the Embarrassed Believer and the church in which he or she participates. The church in the United States cannot genuinely be renewed and serve as a vehicle for revival unless its members witness with the boldness Paul urged on Timothy. And there is also that question of obedience to Christ's command. The Lord did not counsel a shy and mincing faith but a bold embrace of belief in Him, his Father, and the Holy Spirit.

There is widespread paralysis concerning this need for boldness. That paralysis has opened the way for the ersatz "meaning"-mongers, among whom Fulghum, Bly, Redfield, and Williamson are at least physically, if not spiritually, harmless. But the church's failure to contend vigorously for the mind and the soul, and to do so publicly with a strong and defensible claim for truth, opens up a gap in the lives of millions. The Embarrassed Believer is silent, and silence is a condition that does not last long in modern America. The quiet has been displaced by a cacophony of voices, each one selling a different, non-Christian "meaning."

Not so long ago, there was no quiet in the church but actually quite a lot of noise. The noise was a shouting match between various Christian denominations. That's pretty much gone now. I, for one, long for the return of that debate. In fact, any debate among competing, historically tested orthodoxies would be welcomed. I'm even nostalgic for the grating presence of Madalyn Murray O'Hair. She provoked, at least. Now she's skipped town, apparently fleeing the IRS.

Now, instead of denominational slugfests of consequence, we have this parade of seers and tricked-up mystics combining low-brow Eastern slogans with Western marketing. It's just dreamy. Christianity, once a glorious cause with great ambitions for America, is in danger of becoming a museum piece.

So, how to inspire an Embarrassed Believer? First, I think we have to chart how we got into this predicament of an enfeebled church and a confused culture. Then we've got to argue the case for boldness. After all, if timidity has no cost, why bother changing it? If, on the other hand, the stakes are high, if the silencing of Christian belief has placed us on a course with a trajectory that is awful in its results, perhaps then boldness can grow roots. And if a case can be made to challenge the Embarrassed Believer, how does he or she retool or energize faith? What's it mean, anyway, to be a confident, bold believer?

Those who are not Christians do not have to fear a resurgent confidence in Christian belief. In fact, the opposite is true. Ask yourself, was the destruction of confident Christianity and proud communities of deep faith accompanied by a rise in the quality of life? Could the collapse of the quality of life in fact be connected to the cowing of the Christian faithful?

Obviously, I answer yes. This project is a prod to Christians to be Christians, proudly and, if need be, defiantly. It is not a call to a particular politics or platform. Rather, it is an extended argument that any belief shorn of the confidence to live it publicly is not a belief at all but a posture. And postures are easily overwhelmed—and have been.

Some may think that in the aftermath of the October 1997 Washington, D.C., Promise Keepers rally, "Stand in the Gap," a concern over Embarrassed Believers is hardly timely. The gathering of a million committed Christians for a public display of faith is in fact encouraging and may prove to be the critical spark that took a renewal movement and made it a revival, or an awakening.

But the problem of the Embarrassed Believer is the problem of faith apart from the mass rally, faith apart from Sunday church, faith apart from the small prayers of Bible-study groups. It's the problem of living faith in the overwhelmingly secularized day-to-day life of America. To march with millions is an act of commitment but not necessarily an act of courage. To announce to your neighbors and coworkers that you went, you prayed, you sang, and you worshiped—that's the act of courage that completes the act of commitment. As the Promise Keepers attendees witness in that way, and as the tens of millions of American Christians who were not there or who would never dream of participating in such a mass display of belief do so as well, then and only then will the problem of the Embarrassed Believer be remedied.

No sooner did the Promise Keeper phenomenon capture the attention of the secular media, however, than the attempt to whittle it down began. The predictable criticisms from marginal critics—in numbers and in agenda, the National Organization for Women is objectively marginal—did not surprise and do not deter. But the reaction of the elites around the country was telling.

No magazine more perfectly captures the collective consciousness of the opinion elite than *The New Republic.* Even in its studied anti-PC posture, TNR is the busy reader's guide to the dominant opinion of the opinion elite. A week after the Promise Keepers rally, the sub-headline on the magazine mocked the rally: "Christian He-men Hold a Hug-in." There it was. The sneer that has defined the antireligious party for two generations. It is the challenge that sneer presents that is the challenge that every Embarrassed Believer must confront. The table of contents to the issue picked up on the theme. "Promise Keepers: How burly conservatives became sissies" was the title and description given to the report from the Mall. Hanna Rosin's piece followed the predictable line of a confused and frightened secularist:

> The Promise Keepers . . . fill their fists full of Kleenex. They describe their rebirth with schoolgirl giddiness, using words like 'awesome' and 'neat.'

Having deftly laid down a diverting argument, Rosin then rushed off to chastise Republicans. The article, like hundreds of others written by nonbelievers about believers, simply could not suspend its author's consuming, indeed unconscious, antireligious bias. Mockery followed by avoidance of the argument is the standard response.

Not all elite media trashed the Promise Keepers. Matt Labash, a staff writer at the *Weekly Standard,* produced a well-balanced, searching account of the organization, its growth, its leadership, and its theology. His article, in the October 6, 1997, edition, did not spare PK the rod. In fact, some of the darts Labash threw were pretty sharp. ("In many of the conferences," he wrote, "the whole place can degenerate into a heaving, sobbing mass of quivering love handles shaking their way out of the lime-green golf knits.") But Labash covered the

organization *completely,* in the round, and found much to praise
and encourage.

Contrast the Labash approach with that of Rosin's, or more
importantly, with that of *Time,* perhaps the most powerful voice of
all the elite media in terms of reach and lasting impact on American
opinion. Michael G. Maudlin, the managing editor of *Christianity
Today,* reviewed *Time's* coverage, and while he concluded that the
news weekly had "tried hard to be neutral," he was obliged to note
that the magazine could not escape a "tone of foreboding," a tone
"not linked to the particular mission of PK. Rather PK is evangelis-
tic. We are an ominous force because we want people to believe what
we believe about Jesus Christ." Maudlin is exactly right, and he's
right as well about his next observation. *Time's* "sense of foreboding
is entirely missing from *Time's* following cover story on the growth
of Buddhism in America."

Returnees from the PK conference or any other religious event
must be prepared to cope either with this false sense of alarm or with
mockery or with the silence, and not just from small-circulation
magazines with an appeal to a narrow audience of elites or with the
occasional shot from the national news weeklies. Christians at the
dawn of the new millennium are generally prepared for none of
those things. But there are ways to change that and compelling reasons for doing so soon.

The Destruction of Belief

In 1951, longshoreman-philosopher Eric Hoffer published a book titled *The True Believer*. Though much admired by conservatives, Hoffer's title quickly passed into the language as a gentle synonym for a religious fanatic. "True believers" also came to be understood as including primarily the religious—at least those among the faithful sufficiently devout to evidence faith's effects on everyday living.

H. L. Mencken had already plowed the field of antireligious bigotry. It is probably Mencken, more than anyone else, who made hostility to faith almost obligatory among American intellectuals and, more crucially, among American journalists. What had in the U.S. long been an alliance between faith and intellect—between reason and revelation—became at first a split, then a chasm. Today it is a battle. Intellectual elites have never been so far removed from the normal distribution of religious attachment or practice as they are today. And no segment of the intellectual elite is more estranged from faith, and specifically from Christianity, than the media elite—the collection of professionals who write, edit, program, or produce the nation's prestige media: the *New York Times*, the *Washington Post*, the *Los Angeles Times*, the *Christian Science Monitor*, the *Wall Street Journal*, *Time*, *Newsweek*, *U.S. News & World Report*, *Fortune*, *Forbes*, *Business Week*, *Harper's*, *Atlantic*, the *Nation*, the *New Republic*, the *Weekly Standard*, the *New York Review of Books*, *Commentary*, the *American Spectator*, CBS, ABC, NBC, CNN, Fox, PBS, and the major movie studios.

The prestige media is populated by professionals who by and large share a sense of their own significance and their own wisdom. We are, collectively, the opinion leaders.

I say "we" because I am one of them. My credentials are impeccably elite because, of all the self-regarding media centers, I work for PBS, which simply cannot be trumped when it comes to its own high opinion of itself. Ditto my Harvard degree. It's hard to out-posture a Crimson-certified talking head. While my University of Michigan law degree is slightly less valued than, say, one from Yale, its combination with my resumé puts me at the top of the overclass: law clerk on the U.S. Court of Appeals to the D.C. Circuit, ghost writer for Richard Nixon, White House lawyer for Reagan, presidential and gubernatorial appointee to various jobs. My writing has appeared in major papers, and I've guested on the triple crown of network talk shows: *Today*, *Nightline*, and *The Larry King Show*, as well as slumming on *Geraldo* and other book-tour byways.

I'm forty-two, and since picking up the pen for Richard Nixon in 1979, I've been comfortably building my niche in the elite media. It beats working. The only problem is that I am surrounded by people who, upon learning that I am a true believer in Christianity, treat that part of me as either a charming lunacy or an irrelevant eccentricity. The opinion class quite simply doesn't believe in much at all, and certainly not in Christianity. As one political activist told me, in a blunt statement of what I gather most nonbelievers must conclude, he treats my religious belief as an expression of a need for community that is praiseworthy. (That I might be offended by that statement did not cross his mind.)

This condition of the opinion elite can be traced in part to Eric Hoffer.

Hoffer's little book was targeted directly at the opinion class. This was a smaller target in 1951 than it is today, but Hoffer locked on to its collective vanity and scored with a "we/they" tone. Fans of Hoffer could see themselves as the opposite of the "True Believer." Hoffer's readers were the *non*-joiners. The *non*-believers. And although Hoffer had harsh words for intellectuals, he carved out a space where his readers could stand and feel good about themselves. The space he hollowed out has grown larger and larger and larger over the nearly fifty years since he wrote. It is now filled to the very brim with the opinion class. They are best understood as the opposite of what Hoffer held up for criticism.

As the fiftieth anniversary of the publication of *The True Believer* approaches, new editions will inevitably appear. A quick survey of some of Hoffer's recurring points will serve here; but to understand the devastating impact this book had, you ought to read it in its entirety. Here are some representative excerpts from *The True Believer*:[1]

People with a sense of fulfillment think it is a good world and would like to conserve it as it is while the frustrated favor radical change.

Those who would transform a nation . . . must know how to kindle and fan an extravagant hope.

Faith in a holy cause is to a considerable extent a substitute for the lost faith in ourselves.

The religious character of the Bolshevik and Nazi revolutions is generally recognized. The hammer and sickle and the swastika are in a class with the cross. The ceremonial of their parades is as the ceremonial of a religious procession. They have articles of faith, saints, martyrs and holy sepulchers. The Bolshevik and Nazi revolutions are also full-blown nationalist movements. The Nazi revolution had been so from the beginning, while the nationalism of the Bolsheviks was a late development.

Zionism is a nationalist movement and a social revolution. To the orthodox Jew it is also a religious movement. Irish nationalism has a deep religious tinge. The present mass movements in Asia are both nationalistic and revolutionary.

A rising mass movement attracts and holds a following not by its doctrine and promises but by the refuge it offers from the anxieties, barrenness and meaninglessness of an individual existence.

The true believer is without wonder and hesitation.

It was the temporal sword that made Christianity a world religion. Conquest and conversion went hand in hand, the latter often serving

1. Excerpts are from Eric Hoffer, *The True Believer: Thoughts on the Nature of Mass Movements* (New York: Harper & Row, 1951).

as justification and a tool for the former. Where Christianity failed to gain or retain the backing of state power, it achieved neither a wide nor a permanent hold.

Missionary zeal seems . . . an expression of some deep misgivings, some pressing feeling and insufficiency at the center.

Hoffer targeted the very idea of belief—in anything. These excerpts illustrate that as he savaged mass movements he did not spare religious movements. If anything, Hoffer was hardest on Christianity:

At a certain stage, men of words are ready to become timeservers and courtiers. Jesus Himself might not have preached a new Gospel had the dominant Pharisees taken Him into the fold, called Him Rabbi, and listened to Him with deference. A bishopric conferred on Luther at the right moment might have cooled his ardor for a Reformation.

This very influential book, then, hammered on religious belief as the *equivalent* of Nazism and Bolshevism. With great skill and superb writing, Hoffer lumped all believers together and maligned them even as he warned about them. And while launching scathing attack after attack against all believers in anything, he enshrined as a goal a studied detachment from all beliefs. Allegiance was, to Hoffer then and to the opinion elite now, an absurd and dangerous condition. Detachment, preferably a detachment equipped with a wry tone and an unfailing sense of irony, was the ideal!

Poor Hoffer. The result of his work and the work of those like him is a cult of nonbelief headquartered in the offices of major media. He may not have intended to assist in such a transformation. In the middle of his book, he admits that "it is a book of thoughts and it does not shy away from half-truths so long as they seem to hint at a new approach and help to formulate new questions." Perhaps he intended only to shock. But he helped set in motion or at least accelerated a battering of belief.

I doubt many disbelievers will trace their detachment to Eric Hoffer. Vast numbers of them will never even have heard of him. But everywhere around us are the evidences of the passionate distrust of belief that Hoffer embraced and popularized at a time when mass culture was just witnessing the birth of an opinion elite whose visible influence would spread across the country.

Beliefs of all sorts have crumbled in the U.S. in the second half of this century. Hoffer's book was only part of an assault that came from many directions. Those who had believed, however briefly, in Lenin found themselves pursued by the anticommunists and then pummeled by Khrushchev himself via the "secret speech" wherein he detailed Stalin's crimes. And Hoffer was, of course, not alone in his assault on religion. Right-wing idol Ayn Rand, for example, was one of many who joined in the pummeling of traditional Christian values. As the pace of change in the U.S. accelerated—some of it long overdue, as in the dismantling of segregation—the steady drumbeat of criticism of tradition in general continued. Christianity, however, was clearly part of a past that came under a skeptical gaze from most quarters. By the late '60s, much of the old order had been swept away.

The opinion elite rushed to join the nonbelievers, in fact led the charge in many cases, especially within academia and the media. The idea of vigorous belief in anything took a beating. It is impossible to be on the wrong side of history when you're not on any side. The last time the American overclass threw in with a belief, it was the belief in Camelot, and that belief brought with it culpability for a disastrous war in southeast Asia. Thereafter among the opinion elite there would be much sympathy for serious problems but very little prescription on how to solve them.

The opinion elite at century's end is now quick to identify ills and problems, plagues and disturbing trends. But it will not hint at remedies. An air of "professional detachment" from political movements or ideological programs is now deeply rooted in the opinion elite. When strong recommendations are made, they are typically of the sort that urge greater "citizen involvement," "more dialogue and less shouting," "consensus building," or "the politics of the center." Rarely, if ever, will the opinion elite recommend and rally around anything remotely approaching controversy. Campaign against cigarettes? Sure. Campaign against premarital sex? Well, that's a value judgment.

The editors, producers, columnists, anchors, and reporters are fairly sure they are the smartest group around, but they could not be convicted on explicit evidence of believing in anything in particular except perhaps a vague hostility to conservative politics and traditional Christianity.

They are not true believers in anything. And they are committed only to the defeat of true believers who are, for the most part, readily identifiable — in church. (Two notable exceptions are Fred Barnes and Terry Eastland, two political commentators who are frequently on the tube and are also explicit in their faith convictions. Perhaps there are others; if so, their faith is deeply camouflaged.)

Most Christians at the higher levels of Christian publishing and ministry know that the opinion elite is deeply hostile toward Christianity. If they have not personally encountered mockery or indifference, they have heard of it. And most are not angry but genuinely puzzled. "Why is there this attitude of contempt?" is a pretty good summary of the leadership's bewilderment.

I have tried out a number of answers. Two are the most persuasive.

The first is that the implications of real belief are pretty horrific to an opinion class practiced at tolerance but uncomfortable with any verbal condemnation. If God exists and sin exists, sin needs to be named, even if we do not presume to legislate against sin.

Members of the opinion elite are not prepared to risk the sort of unpopularity that results from explicit principles and explicit condemnations.

In other words, it's not that the believers are wrong. It's a fear that they are right.

And then there is the problem of pride.

If God exists and has become incarnate in Christ and accessible through Scripture, then everyone is of equal value. The truly radical egalitarians are Christians, and the ideas of celebrity and significance, the twin bumpers of anchors, editors, and other stars of the media elite, don't mean much to radical egalitarians.

I have only two extended excerpts from Scripture in this book. The first is the concluding remarks of God to Job, which appear in chapter 16. The second is the entire Book of Ecclesiastes, which is included as the Appendix. I include this book of the Bible because, even though the Bible is so easily obtained and indeed is widely read in some circles, among the opinion elite it is not likely to be close at hand; and I want to make Ecclesiastes impossible to avoid, especially for this group of readers.

Ecclesiastes is a book about the effects of time. It is particularly invaluable in *our* times, and it ought to be required reading for every would-be member of any of the country's elites, and certainly the media elite. In the first chapter of Ecclesiastes the author wrote, "I saw all the deeds that are done under the sun; and see, all is vanity and a chasing after wind" (1:14 NRSV). He continued:

I said to myself, "I have acquired great wisdom, surpassing all who were over Jerusalem before me; and my mind has had great experience of wisdom and knowledge." And I applied my mind to know wisdom and to know madness and folly. I perceived that this also is but a chasing after wind. (1:16–17 NRSV)

"A chasing after wind" is one of the most marvelous phrases in the entire Bible. It provides the perfect picture of futility. It conveys the fruitlessness of attempting to capture that which cannot be captured— to possess what by definition cannot be possessed.

And it nicely sums up what has come to serve as the substitute for belief. Faith in God has cratered in America. It has hit bottom. Not dead, but invisible and fading in significance. In its place has developed an almost ludicrous self-importance that leads to movie stars and singers addressing university communities—Barbra Streisand at Harvard University's Kennedy School of Government, Alec Baldwin thumping for campaign reform—while talking heads debate "critical race theory." Once the respectability of belief was challenged, the easily cowed ran for cover. And in the wake of the society-wide retreat from belief, a substitute followed that has been wholly unsatisfactory.

T he process of forgetting is well-advanced even before an event com-
mences. So many interesting and compelling stories and people
have crossed our minds' paths to this moment that no matter how
momentous the occasion just around the bend, it will be immediately
under the pressure of the combined impacts of all that came before it
and the awesome anticipation of all that is yet to come. Thus the very
idea of capturing significance for a measurable period of time is
laughable.

Significance at least seemed possible in premodern times. When
Henry of Bolingbroke returned from exile in France to wrest power
from and eventually execute Richard II, an entire country—and
indeed, a continent—watched with fascination. And when his son,
Henry V, made successful war against France and triumphed at
Agincourt, there was again the illusion of significance for Henry and
his generals. When Joan of Arc arrived at the Dauphin's court a few
years later to lead the turn of history against the English, then her significance began to crowd out that of the two Henrys. And so it continued throughout the fifteenth century—a parade of powerful,
charismatic individuals, each one in turn cornering history's attention
for a moment.

A century later, it was Luther and Calvin and Henry VIII and
Elizabeth taking their turns. And a few decades later it was Louis XIV
and Marlborough, and then Maria Theresa, then George III, then
Washington, then Napoleon, then Victoria and Disraeli and
Gladstone, then the Kaiser and the Tsar, then Lenin and Wilson, then
Stalin, Churchill, FDR, and Hitler, then . . .

The point is that in a historical blink of an eye, Churchill will be as
familiar to the world as Henry of Bolingbroke is to us.

All of recorded history is but an apostrophe against measurable time

that has already elapsed. Infinite time, of course, crushes into nothing-
ness—even the vast number of years since the Big Bang (the event we
Christians call *creation*). The only guarantee in this book is that this
book and all other books will eventually be forgotten if not absolutely
destroyed. So why write it?

Or why labor to create nature preserves or wilderness areas? We
know—intellectually—that eventually these areas of near-pristine
nature will be destroyed. Cataclysmic climatic change will eventually
arrive, whether advanced or retarded by humankind's efforts.
Eventually, it is all dust. So why bother?

These are the sorts of questions that arise when one reads history as
a hobby, as I do. Some folks play golf every week or collect stamps or
hike. I read. Usually popular history.

That habit, which is an acquired taste that I developed only after
three decades of other pastimes, has a few curious by-products. First, it's
actually difficult to take very seriously the grander pronouncements of
American politics. And it's very hard to take *anything* very seriously—
except theology and theology's subject, God. Because nothing else lasts.
And because nothing else provides significance, order, and explanation. Further, to borrow loosely from Henry Kissinger, good theology
has the additional benefit of being true.

It is easy to convince most people of the negative half of my argument: the ultimate insignificance of all that goes on around them.
Some of that recognition is instinctive in well-balanced people. Movie
superstar Tom Hanks reflected on his celebrity status when *That Thing
You Do* debuted in the summer of 1996: "The '90s, to me, have been—
it seems like I've rarely been able to get out of this white hot spotlight.
Which *is* really fun, for a period of time. Then after a while it becomes
just white-hot. It gets to be a little bit uncomfortable. If you're not ana-
lyzing why you're there, then you will just assume that it's never going
to go away—or that you deserve it in the first place. And no one
deserves this much attention. No one does."

Hanks is right. No one deserves that much attention. And eventually, no one gets that much attention.

"They don't want me anymore," sang Norma Desmond in the wonderful song from *Sunset Boulevard,* "With One Look." "They all say I'm

through," she lamented. And "they" were right—and not just in the movie or the play *Sunset Boulevard.* All fame fades.

Perhaps you agree. But the second part of my point—that only theology and theology's subject, God, can provide significance, order, and an explanation—is much more implausible, especially today when folks like Hoffer have roared around for nearly fifty years laying out an indictment of all belief systems and especially Christianity. In recent years, the general havoc wreaked on the idea of belief has been supported by celebrity-seeking academics organized into the Jesus Seminar as well as by a host of political activists who find the commands of Scripture inconveniently clear. The Embarrassed Believer knows just how hostile the terrain has become.

The constant assault on the idea of belief is absolutely necessary to those threatened by belief. The reason? The awful but obvious insignificance of modern life is hard to deny for very long. The illusion of significance is pretty easily shattered by anyone with a decent gift for argument. And since it is so easy to prove meaninglessness and insignificance, individuals will want to ask how to find the genuine article. Of course, the genuine article is God; but God requires belief. And once belief is obtained, obedience follows, and obedience requires change; and all of a sudden, inconvenient and often unpleasant sacrifices must be made.

If we ever take God seriously in this country—really, really take God seriously—imagine the changes that would follow. None of them would be compelled by law, mind you. That is a bogeyman invented by the enemies of belief: the idea of an absolutist preacher-pastor-president banning beer and banking and barbecues. No, any changes would be compelled not by law but by a serious belief in the necessity of personal obedience to a God who demands what He has always demanded. If that obedience became generalized, the changes would be momentous. Which is why opponents of those changes must fight tooth and nail against the resurrection of belief.

But the opponents have a problem. The current trajectory of the country and its culture is so bad, the conditions of modern life so awful, that belief is breaking out again.

For the Embarrassed Believer, the last few years have been a tonic, an energizing and refreshing wind of change. Scores of younger men and women have assessed the spiritual poverty of the country and the emptiness of their own lives and have found their way back to Christ. Many have found their way into a church. Now they must find their way into the culture at large.

The Trajectory

3

Let me put out a little bit more of Hoffer at this point to buttress my method. About a third of the way through his manuscript, he paused and noted that

> the reader is expected to quarrel with much that is said in this part of the book. He is likely to feel that much has been exaggerated and much ignored. But this is not an authoritative text book. It is a book of thoughts, and it does not shy away from half-truths so long as they seem to hint at a new approach and help formulate new questions. (*The True Believer,* Harper & Row, 1951)

"To illustrate a principle," says Hoffer, "you must exaggerate much and you must omit much!"

Already many of my readers may be disagreeing with my direction, especially if the reader is part of or admires the American media. But we cannot afford to be polite or subtle. As the century and the millennium draw to a close, we must be blunt. "He who has ears to hear, let him hear," Christ said in Matthew's Gospel when He wanted His audience to focus. As we begin to examine the collapse of Christian witness, the defense of belief, and the urgent need for Christians to now declare and defend their faith, we need to focus on what their absence from the larger culture has meant. While I do not need to "exaggerate much" to make my arguments, there is neither space nor need to include the lengthy statistical summaries that undergird the assertions in this chapter.

The most obvious fact about the U.S. at the end of the millennium is that it is a deeply diseased country. In slightly more than fifty years it has plummeted from a stable and ordered society with problems that needed corrections (segregation and rural poverty, for examples) to a society of routine violence and deep pathology.

Listen. There are lots of books and studies out there if you need proof. Violent crime involving the threat or actual occasion of serious injury skyrocketed in the past generation. The number of children born to unwed parents—an undeniable burden on the kids that can and does routinely ruin lives—now approaches one out of three births, up from one out of thirty only three decades ago. Legal abortion, largely unknown in 1960, now ends one out of four pregnancies. Drug use and sexual activity among youth is at an extraordinary level, and pornography of the basest sort is widely available in every corner video store.

Call me old-fashioned, but things aren't so good.

There's a group of professional skeptics who would love to argue each of these assertions, who would challenge my tone as judgmental or alarmist. At a recent conference, one academic dismissed my unremarkable catalog of factual assertions as a "Jeremiad." I do not bother to respond to the implication that my conclusions are somehow hysterical or overwrought. Believers have wasted far too many years arguing the obvious. The situation is *not* good. The trajectory is worse.

The most obvious thing in the world is that evil now dominates the culture. Hold a debate if you want, but fools and only fools can conclude that we do not have to worry about the escalation of evil. Of course the U.S. at millennium's end is not Hitler's Germany or Stalin's Soviet Union. But the soul-destroying forces of modern America—violence, fear, lust, addiction—have shattered tens of millions of lives and are claiming more. Debating whether the trends are positive or negative is about as silly as debating the proposition that cars are faster now than they were in the '30s.

A small but telling example:

When in 1996 the television industry dodged a clear demand from the public to institute a ratings system that would alert parents to content, a senior writer for *TV Guide* appeared on my television show to defend the industry's decision. When I suggested that the television producers could not be trusted to rate their own shows, I offered up *Friends* as a show the industry had judged suitable for fourteen-year-olds.

Sex outside of marriage—indeed, outside of "committed relationships"—is to *Friends* as water was to the old *Flipper* TV show. Sex is part of every *Friends* episode, and indeed there would be no show at all except for the constant focus on the sex lives of the leads. The behavior that is modeled to a fourteen-year-old viewer is this: Move to the big city and get a lover or many lovers as soon as possible.

From watching *Friends*, a fourteen-year-old might reasonably conclude that sex outside of marriage is not only tolerable, it's great. The producers might argue that no fourteen-year-olds have sex on the show. True enough, but totally beside the point. The show sells sex. Should a fourteen-year-old watch it? I argued to the critic that the idea the show was appropriate for fourteen-year-olds was laughable.

My friend from *TV Guide* chided me. Of course the PG-14 rating was correct. "C'mon," he said, "it's the '90s."

It is the '90s. Compare the '90s to the '50s using any value system you want. Is crime more or less prevalent now or then? Teen sexuality and pregnancy? Drug use among adults or youth? Depression or other serious mental illness? Fear? Hatred? Evil? It is true that one evil is gone; government sponsored racial segregation is no more. But while that undeniably good thing has occurred, have the last thirty years brought different races together, or is the poison of racism deeper and more deadly now than at the height of Jim Crow?

Even if you conclude that formal equality between races and between men and women has been achieved since World War II, nearly every other kind of corrosive, soul-killing, dehumanizing evil has exploded over the past fifty years.

So ask yourself: What if the trajectory of the past half-century continues unaltered for another half-century? If the '90s were unimaginable to the people of the '50s, imagine what another few decades will bring—if the trajectory remains the same, that is.

Hello, *Blade Runner*. Do *you* want to go there?

Readers usually rush on without pausing to really ponder such rhetorical questions. But here is one place where I hope my core audience of embarrassed Christians will put down the book and think of a particular response. If the direction of the culture does not change—if violence, drug abuse, and sexual excess, to cite just three indicators, follows the same trend line established in the past thirty years—what do you imagine the country will look like in 2030? Inevitably, folks I pose this question to, especially my fellow Christians, know that the answer is a horrible one.

Belief in God makes possible the belief that the trajectory can change. That God can and will redeem lives if individuals ask Him to. But the trajectory does not have to change. In fact, it can alter for the worse. The debauchery and violence that took a half-century to grow can double again in intensity in half the time. The engines of rapid change are everywhere but especially in the little ubiquitous boxes littered about our homes and schools: televisions and computers.

No doubt there are people, even in the church, who think we've already hit bottom. Perhaps you are one of them. Before you get too comfortable with the idea that the conditions can't get any worse—that you can't fall off the floor—ask yourself only if similarly situated folks felt the same way in 1947. A world stunned by the Holocaust told itself that history had bottomed out. The killing fields of Cambodia and Rwanda were thirty and fifty years in the future, respectively.

But there is hope. Huge hope in fact. God is faithful. The trajectory can change. Indeed, it may already have changed.

In the November 17, 1997, issue of *Christianity Today,* the editors used an old device—the list of one hundred—to illustrate a recent development: There is much dynamic Christian ministry at work in the world today, and the editors underlined this by listing one hundred inspiring Christian undertakings of recent months. Each of these examples of faithfulness to the gospel imperatives is an inspiring reminder of the capacity that God-filled people bring to battles against evil.

So, too, is there great hope in youth. I was on the campus of California's Azusa Pacific University in late fall of 1997, and I took the opportunity to attend the students' mandatory morning chapel. "Mandatory" and "college student" are typically not great partners, so I expected a quiet, relatively quick shuffling-in and shuffling-out service.

Almost an hour later I sought out the worship leader, a young senior named Dan, to commend him on his leadership of a service of tremendous energy, integrity, and joy. The guest preacher that day, Erwin McManus, pastors a large, urban church in Los Angeles, and he used the time to exhort the more than one thousand eighteen- to twenty-two-year-olds on the need to summon up courage and strike out into the urban world to minister to the hurting and the lost. The cities, he argued, are the frontiers of Christian witness, and they are dangerous places that desperately needed the commitments of the chapel's attendees.

As I participated in this service and listened to this message, I again understood that, indeed, with God all things are possible. The trajectory *can* change. But even if every one of the graduates of Azusa Pacific takes up that mission, and even if every one of the graduates of Gordon, Eastern, Hope, Wheaton, Westmont, and the dozens of other great Christian colleges do the same, the tide is still flowing strongly against them. The church as a whole must shake off its lethargy, must recover its voice and its boldness.

John J. DiIulio Jr. is a scholar and writer who first publicized the term "the super-predator." The super-predator is the urban youth whose violence is as shocking to suburbia as it is now statistically unremarkable. This is the young criminal whose lack of conscience is so complete that even as courageous a minister and as hopeful an evangelical as Chuck Colson is obliged to shudder at the future peopled with such aging sociopaths.

But DiIulio is also the writer who has committed himself to understanding how the "super-preachers," as he calls them, can and have successfully brought the gospel to young men and women of exactly this sort, how their churches have flourished in the urban chaos that has consumed so many.

The trajectory can change, but only if there are thousands of DiIulios out in America, reading, watching, and eventually, taking action. At present, the numbers are laughably small as compared to any measure of evil. But the ranks could swell, and swell overnight, if the curious could be witnessed to and the converted could be catalyzed to act.

Many obstacles will have to be overcome, too, if the trajectory is to change. The very first one, and perhaps the greatest, is the fear of proclaiming a faith that is greatly mocked or attacked as dangerous. It is not enough to do good works while camouflaging the motivating force of the gospel behind the works. It is not the work that changes the world and turns the trajectory. It is the gospel. That is the paradox. Christians in America trying to save the lost, comfort the suffering, cure the ill, clothe the naked, and bring joy to the despairing will not make a significant and lasting impact unless they do so openly and without apology as Christians. The witness must accompany the work, or the work will not endure.

And the world is hungry for the witness.

The debate had been fairly intense. The crowd of two hundred consisted overwhelmingly of human-relations professionals who were wedded to the amorphous cause of affirmative action. My television studio and the Human Relations Commission of Los Angeles had jointly sponsored a "dialogue" entitled "Beyond Affirmative Action," which turned out not to go very far beyond the issue of the day: Proposition 209—the California Civil Rights Initiative, which became law in 1996. At the time of this debate the controversy surrounding the CCRI had just begun to swirl. It still continues to swirl.

The discussion had been civil, but the views of the participants could not be reconciled. And following a too-long two hours of back and forth, we adjourned.

There's a space in time that follows all such forums. It is the courtesy zone, wherein no matter how sharp the exchange or how deep the disagreement, the participants mix and mingle and smile and acknowledge that, after all, it's just a forum. Watch C-SPAN to the end of any given program, and you will see that this milling around follows nearly every presentation.

A cardinal rule of the courtesy zone is that the debate ought not to carry over into it. Certainly no new or taxing subjects should be introduced. "Give it a break" is the motto. The weary participants, after all, deserve their getaway to unfold unmolested.

Well, after this particular verbal twelve-rounder, the executive director of the commission, Christopher McCauly, came up smiling broadly, grabbed my hand, and gave me an intense look. "I'm really looking forward to your God series," he said. "It will mean a lot to me."

The sudden juxtaposition of an intense affirmative-action debate with my *Searching for God in America* series was jarring. As was this self-disclosure. Lots of folks greet television people with throwaway lines about shows they've watched and enjoyed. But few go out of the way to declare value in that which they haven't yet seen.

I did not inquire at the time why Chris was looking forward to the shows. More than a month passed, but I continued to ask myself why he would care and why he would tell me he cared. Finally I called him at his office to ask why he thought he was going to enjoy it. When he returned the call, he said that in the last year he had experienced a personal religious renewal. Through All Saints Episcopal Church in Pasadena, he had begun to search for God, and he had come 180 degrees in his relationship with God. Thus his interest in the series: It was arriving on the air not long after he had arrived back in church.

Another story. As election '96 began to heat up in the spring of that year, my friend Bill Press—now of *Crossfire* fame and a hopeless, if amiable, lefty—decided to pitch television stations in the Los Angeles market on the idea of a right-left commentary segment. The first station we targeted was channel 9, KCAL-TV. One week into the discussions, Bill landed the *Crossfire* job and moved to D.C. But KCAL still wanted to talk, so I made my way in early March to the restaurant on the Paramount Studio lot to meet the station's political producer, Lisa Eichenberger.

We were at lunch for two hours, and except for the first twenty minutes, the subjects were God, religion, American spirituality, and the rise of belief. Lisa is herself a Presbyterian but also an enthusiastic proponent of *The Celestine Prophecy,* a book—as I've already argued—the very commercial success of which underscores America's search for the transcendent even as its content drags millions away from the path to genuine faith. Once again, my *Searching* experience had allowed a conversation to open a door that is normally barred, and two people who had never met before, both working in the business renowned for its hard edges and standoffishness, were deep into a conversation about God. In all fairness, the accelerated intimacy of the conversation was helped along by our discovery that Lisa was a great friend of, and had been maid of honor in the wedding of, a man with whom I had passed hundreds of hours of friendship in high school. But, as Lisa said, such meetings are not accidents.

Of course the reaction of two people to a pending television series and its host hardly makes a statistically significant sampling. But this reaction was part of the general response of strangers to the title and the subject matter of *Searching for God in America*. That pattern suggests a reason is behind it all.

Take my university faculty. I teach at Chapman University Law School in Orange County, California. As part of the life of the university, faculty members give talks to each other concerning their recent work. I was asked to deliver such a talk, and I titled it "Searching for God with PBS" and included a bite-size summary of the series. The room was set up for an ordinary attendance, but the provost and I were soon carrying in chairs to meet demand. And the faculty was intrigued. The dozen questions that followed my thirty-minute talk were not the polite thank-you-for-coming variety but rather variations on the theme What did it mean? What were all these religious people telling you? Is another Great Awakening upon us? Ought that to upset us?

The faculty forum was just another episode in the now nearly three-year-old series of questions I've encountered as a result of taking the subject of God seriously. Who's buying these Deepak Chopra books by the zillions? Who's showing up at the Promise Keeper rallies? Why are these megachurches going mega? Is there significance to the end of the millennium? What's all this New Age stuff? Is Jesus God? Is Mohammed a prophet? Why is Islam advancing? What's the *Tibetan Book of Dying*? I'm worried about my kids; should I join a church?

How do I know God is real?

A friend suggested to me that *SFGA* was an expanded version of a late-night gabfest among college sophomores lost in the search for the meaning of life. He was right. That's exactly what it was. But the sophomores are now in their thirties, forties, and fifties or older, and they want to continue the conversation. I have to conclude that everyone enjoys the conversation, even if he or she never went to college and never argued about whether God exists.

Here's what's going on, I think. It is particularly important for believers to understand that a time of great opportunity for evangelism is opening up—has opened up. Here's why.

The twin illusions of control and significance are shattered beyond repair.

The illusion of control allowed its believers in America and beyond to hold the idea that hard work and moral living would yield happiness.

But they often don't. Rabbi Harold Kushner, author of *When Bad Things Happen to Good People* and a guest on my series, forcefully assaulted this myth in his recounting of the tragic death of his young son. In fact, evil and tragedy are everywhere around us, and it is getting harder not to notice. Practically everyone who has reached the age of forty has directly experienced unfair suffering.

The idea of American omnipotence was an unspoken assumption of the youth of most baby boomers. There were enemies, certainly; but we could outthink and outspend even the combined force of the Soviets and the communist Chinese. While Vietnam shattered the faith of many younger people in America's purpose, it did not dent the underlying assumption about the country's power. It was American omnipotence that repulsed so many among the antiwar crowd. And on the other side—the Silent Majority side of the street—the discontent was not that America lacked the ability, the power, to run the world but that it lacked the will. Both sides could agree at least that the country was a superpower of almost unlimited resources.

This belief supported not just the Vietnam expedition but the Great Society, the Apollo program, the explosion of the higher education imperative, and the Americanization of global culture as well. The idea that talent, wealth, and smarts could control the future seeped into everyone's outlook. Hubris was to American life what fluoride became to American water.

Even as the illusion of control took root, the other grand illusion, the illusion of significance, allowed its adherents to believe in enduring contributions and the stability of influence or power. The rapidity of decline and the suddenness of power and taste shifts clobbered this one years ago. Some politicians still labor under the misapprehension that they matter in the long haul. But if the collapse of the Soviet Union and the fall of the Berlin Wall stand for anything, it is for the proposition that nothing human lasts for very long, even when backed by totalitarian force. The acceleration of obsolescence is marked, and the age of the Internet is the age of zero controls.

Once the beliefs in the possibilities of control and significance blew up, the rise in the interest in spirituality was inevitable. Set aside our Christian beliefs. Approach the situation as any intelligent agnostic might. If nothing matters and nothing lasts and there are no guarantees, then what gives life meaning? Mere reproduction? Even those who deeply love their children intuitively know there's got to be more.

The quest for that "more" is what powered the interest in *SFGA*. Sort of. But not wholly. Anyone who believes that confusion and chaos in the culture are the only things behind the burgeoning interest in spirituality has bought into a secular response. If you examine that response you will see the quiet, corrosive influence of pseudo-psychology at work in the explanation of spiritual hunger. Folks uncomfortable with the big question about the existence of God hold on to a psychological explanation for the upsurge in wondering. It is an explanation that is plausible for them because it obviously connects the rise of faith with a "rational" explanation for all this praying.

But there is another explanation as well. *Star Trek* fans know of the potency of the tractor beam. When the Klingons wished to pull an unsuspecting earth-craft into their range, the tractor beam went on. When the starship *Enterprise* needed to retrieve its small command vehicles, its tractor beam went on. Tractor beams were invisible rays that acted as retractable grappling hooks.

High concept: God's got a tractor beam, and He's flipped the switch. It's working. We are collectively drawing close to Him. Some of us are aware of this and want to know what's up. Others are unaware . . . for now.

The risk I take in writing the preceding two paragraphs is that the highbrows among Embarrassed Believers abandon this book the moment this first, less-than-serious device arrives on the printed page. Effective imaging doesn't work for them if it's insufficiently highbrow, and *Star Trek* will not do. Give 'em some lines from Sufi mystic Rumi that are impenetrable without a decade of training, and that'll hold their attention, but not *Star Trek*.

But the tractor beam is exactly the answer that fits any theology and the only explanation that can unify the similar reactions of tremendously dissimilar people. Insecurity is indeed on the rise. Absolutely. But that need not compel a rise in the interest in spirituality. To say so would overestimate the relative insecurity of our age compared with, say, living in Paris in 1791. I am not aware of any great spiritual awakening during the Reign of Terror.

On the other hand, if God does exist and He's upped the power of His call on His people a notch or two, well then, all sorts of hard-to-explain things make sense.

How does the mortar get sucked out from between the bricks of a Berlin Wall?

How does a Middle East long rent by insolvable conflicts find and hold on to a genuine progress toward peace, even in the face of horrible stresses such as have marked Jerusalem in the past two years?

Why do books on angels fly off the shelves? Why did tens of thousands journey to Medjugore in the former Yugoslavia in the belief that the mother of a Man born two thousand years ago is appearing there regularly to children?

Why do acquaintances you've known for decades reveal that recently they've started attending a weekly Bible study?

How does a movement like the Promise Keepers put a million people on the Mall in October 1997?

Of course there are still tremendous horrors in the world. The killing fields of Bosnia and Rwanda are just additional reminders that the '90s have produced butchery on a scale with any other time.

But it is impossible to deny real, measurable upticks in concrete evidences of religious belief. I have already mentioned Promise Keepers, the parachurch movement that effortlessly fills stadiums with vast crowds of men in search of spiritual significance and that stunned America with its national gathering in 1997. And an evangelist like the Harvest Crusade's Greg Laurie is addressing immense crowds, including more than sixty-three thousand in Orange County, California's, Anaheim Stadium on July 4, 1996, and an overflow crowd in the same stadium (then under extensive renovation) a year later. And there is the "new church" movement, captured in its intensity and significance by journalist Charles Truehart in the August 1996 issue of the *Atlantic Monthly*:

> The churches are remarkable chiefly for their size. Many of these (mostly Protestant) congregations count thousands of people in attendance on a weekend—in some cases more than 10,000. For their hugeness they are often known, and often chagrined to be known, as megachurches.

Among the other labels one hears are full-service churches, seven-day-a-week churches, pastoral churches, apostolic churches, 'new tribe' churches, new paradigm churches, seeker sensitive churches. No two of these terms mean quite the same thing, but together, like blind men with the elephant, they describe the beast rather well. These very large and dynamic congregations may at the moment number no more than 400, but are the fastest growing ones in the country.

Not even a large raft of statistics will turn some heads. Some cannot allow themselves to focus on the phenomena I've just reeled off. The prospect of the triumph of faith is too upsetting for too many skeptics. Particularly if it grew so close as to compel a personal evaluation of the issue. Very quickly each of these "movements" and many others—the rise of Christian publishing and music, for example—are boxed up and shipped off to the warehouse of untidy facts and surprising/unsettling discoveries.

I am aware of how harsh the judgment of an elite can be, and I've already heard some of that collected judgment denigrating the renewal movement in the U.S. The skeptics are still numerous. The Roman Emperor Julian ought to be their hero. More than sixteen hundred years ago he attempted to reimpose paganism after nearly fifty years of unfettered Christianity. Julian failed. He liked the old system, but the rise of Christianity had crushed it beyond recovery. Christianity prospered even though the empire that first persecuted and then nurtured it collapsed.

And I think any attempt to dismiss the growing spiritual revival outright will fail as well. The tractor beam is too strong. And the need is too great.

No, the real danger to the new revival is not in the skepticism of elites but rather in carnival mysticism: a melange of beliefs and bits of philosophy backed by CDs of Gregorian chant. The "mystical" is, however, very thin. Substance is required, and discipline. Not surprisingly, each of my guests on *SFGA* emphasized rigor in religious practice. More on that later. There are worse things than nonbelief.

But the lesson is obvious. The great churning is well advanced. People want to ask even the most unsophisticated questions and many are increasingly refusing to allow embarrassment at their lack of sophistication to overcome their curiosity. They want to know about God. In fact they want to know God.

The one overwhelming obstacle continues to delay millions. People *are* embarrassed by their desire to know God. Hoffer and his allies past and present have done their work well.

PEOPLE ARE EMBARRASSED TO TALK ABOUT THE DEEP THINGS

This is a question I like to pose to audiences convened for a secular purpose: If, upon repair to a fine French restaurant for dinner with professional colleagues, one of your number proposed a prayer before dining, would you be embarrassed?

My literary agent, Sealy Yates, is one of the very few lawyers I know who asks the Lord's blessing at public meals. My pastors do as well. But, you know, that's their job. Sealy, on the other hand, doesn't have to do it! And whether I'm eating with my agent or eating with my pastors, I'm still not used to prayer in public places.

So I can pose this question without any fear of struttin' my faith, as I'm too much a prisoner of the culture to invoke a grace at public meals though my family does so in the quiet of our dining room. But prayer— obvious prayer—in a restaurant? Well, that's just too embarrassing.

Most folks at the margin of religious belief are acutely embarrassed by the idea of believing in God. Many folks who would profess a very firm faith, myself included, also are embarrassed by too much attention paid to the subject outside of the approved parameters of faith. It is this sense of embarrassment that acts as an obstacle to people's desire to talk about faith in God or God's nature.

If you need proof of this, consider the people in your workplace. How many of them are religious? To which denominations do any of them belong? Ever have a conversation about God with any of them?

More to the point, if you were compelled to ask any of them, "Do you believe in God, and if so, why?" would you feel embarrassed while making the inquiry?

Most readers will have answered yes to the last question. It's unlikely that you know much about your coworkers' belief systems.

The embarrassment associated with belief is nothing other than a reflection of the culture. And it's a relatively recent development.

In March 1996, the *Los Angeles Times* kicked off its spring-training coverage of the Dodgers with the usual spate of articles about new faces in the dugout. One of those, Greg Gagne, a longtime major league shortstop, was profiled as an evangelical Christian. The pattern to the story was fairly predictable: Dissolute youth finds Christ and lives out his faith in an environment generally thought hostile to Christian living—the clubhouse. The headline was a classic of the genre: HEAVEN HELP THOSE WHO UNDERRATE GAGNE.

What I found remarkable about the article was that it is "remarkable" that a major league athlete is a practicing Christian.

Can you hear the conversation between the editor and the writer?

EDITOR: Get me a profile on Gagne. No one in this city can even pronounce his name.

WRITER: Don't know much about him. Oh, yeah, he's a born-againer. Want to run with that?

EDITOR: Sure, why not? Writes itself: "Locker-room leader looks to the Lord for long-ball."

WRITER: Have it for you tomorrow.

Add a few expletives, and that's probably the way many newsroom conversations go about athletes with religious beliefs.

But what's relevant is that in 1996 an athlete's religious belief can still support a whole story. After all, these athlete-Christians are not exactly rare. There are Bible studies throughout most professional leagues. Danny Wuerffel proclaimed his faith after Florida's romp in the Sugar Bowl, and Carolina Panther quarterback Kerry Collins did the same after upsetting the Dallas Cowboys in the NFC playoffs in early 1997. The story line is not new.

But religious faith openly expressed is perceived as slightly bizarre—that's the reason why the story runs, and that's the reason God-talk will still embarrass most ordinary folks and why prayers at restaurants do not approach in volume the number of prayers at dinner in private homes. It is also the reason why superstar Deion Sanders's conversion in 1997 warranted notice but no explanations. In a country starving for any scoop on its celebrities, no secular media outlet I touched on dealt with the specifics of Sanders's turn to faith. I suspect producers dismissed it as either too weird or too dull. In fact, no story would have interested me more, and I suspect millions of others would have agreed.

Two unchurched friends of mine once invited me for a cup of coffee. They had concluded that, because I attended church on a weekly basis and had taught Sunday school, I was the fellow to approach. Their proposal was simple: They wanted to start a Bible study, but they didn't know how. As I didn't belong to such a study, nor had I ever, we had a good laugh over my "expertise" and decided to find a fourth. We agreed to be careful with our search. We wanted no overly enthusiastic believers. Rather, we wanted 'tweeners—folks, like us, between agnosticism and deep faith.

I can't recall who coined the term, but we all agreed that each of us had a problem with the "J-word," that is, *Jesus.* Not a problem in believing in Him. That was the point. We did believe (or almost believed, in one case). But we were not particularly comfortable saying "Jesus" out loud. "Spirituality" is very easy to say. "God" is pretty easy to say. "Lord" is easy to say. "Jesus" is not easy to say. It is especially difficult to say for professionals schooled in decades of secular classrooms, particularly in elite secular classrooms.

Here's my scale of religious terms as they rank on the "easy-to-say" through "hard-to-say" scale, beginning with the easiest:

Spirituality	Lord
Belief system	The Spirit
Religion	The Holy Spirit
Faith	Christ
The Divine	Jesus
God	My Savior

That's a twelve-step program from the amorphous, ambiguous, out-there idea of a Cosmic Something to a theological statement about the relationship between Jesus and the speaker.

The reason some terms are not "easy to say" is because they are identified by the dominant media culture with anti-intellectual fundamentalism. This is the curse of the Scopes Trial, and it is still abroad and strong. Eric Hoffer added fuel to this fire. Norman Lear added to it. Thousands in the intellectual elite in this country wear like a medal this attitude of contempt for Christian belief.

Now, it's one thing to believe. It's another thing to be hooted at for belief. America hasn't produced many religious martyrs in the past couple of generations, but there are huge numbers of believers who have been—who are—insulted for believing. The assumption that stupidity accompanies religious conviction is very deep-seated. In February 1993, the *Washington Post* ran a story on the "Gospel Grapevine" stating—without comment—that politically active Christians were poor, uneducated, and easy to command. The paper retracted the statement the next day, but for a moment the curtain went up on the general attitude of elite media toward belief: It's a yahoo thing.

The television culture of the past thirty years in America has elevated one talent above all others—the rapid, devastating put-down. Witticisms generally are valued. They drive the entire sitcom industry. But the crushing comeback, that's the most honored line of all. The Age of Mockery has dawned as a result, wherein literally nothing—and specifically, preeminently, religious faith—is sacred because nothing is off limits to mockery.

Not surprisingly, the nation that watches an endless amount of television adapts, slowly but surely, to television's values. Super Bowl ads don't cost a half-million bucks a half-minute because they are ineffective. What is honored on the tube is honored by us generally. What is scorned there is scorned by us generally. What is missing there is missing generally among us. And as the ability to deliver scornful remarks has become valued on the small screen, it has become valued within the culture at large.

Now, television itself does not often overtly mock faith. I argued in the introduction to *Searching for God in America* that television simply ignores the subject.

But even while shunning God, television does elevate such practices as the snappy one-liner. And in modeling this method of conversation, television has telegraphed as well two best techniques to avoid becoming a target: First, play offense. Roseanne gives as good as she gets. It is hard to recall Don Rickles being abused. Second, defend nothing wholeheartedly. If you are uncommitted in all aspects of modern life, you can hardly be a target. The position of ironic detachment from everything is the usual stance of television's heroes. What's more, it is the preferred air of nearly every "elite" journalist I know.

And this is almost the reverse of historian Herbert Butterfield's injunction: Cling absolutely to Christ, and to all other things be relatively committed. Christians and other believers are supposed to be the very opposite of detached. But attachment has a cost.

People hate to be embarrassed. It is often worse than being cheated and worse than most other minor victimizations. Embarrassment is terrible because it generally involves some element of personal culpability. If you are being hooted at, it is likely you had a hand in setting yourself up.

Given that we know that religious belief is an open invitation to mockery, why telegraph the vulnerability? And given that the culture as a whole is well schooled in the vicious verbal sucker-punch, why ask for it by bringing up the subject of God?

Recall the idea of praying at a restaurant? I think most people cringe at the idea because they fear what the complete stranger at the next table will think: *Holy Roller alert!* It's not embarrassment about faith but fear of attribution of mindless zealotry or Elmer Gantryism that sends the red into the cheeks.

The prayer-in-restaurants dilemma is only one easy-to-understand example of how embarrassment inhibits expressions of interest in God. It's not just believers who understand how embarrassing belief can be. It's seekers as well. In fact, who better to understand the potential for scorn than one who has himself heaped such abuse on a target? The seeker who has scorned believers as stupid or weird is going to be acutely aware of what others will think if this belief stuff gets out of hand, if an encounter with Christ changes his or her own life.

If embarrassment is not an obstacle to your inquiry, fine. Congratulations. But keep a check on your pride. I've been scolded by some Christians who think embarrassment in a Christian is somehow an impossibility—an admission of unauthentic faith. This attitude is not only non-biblical, it's downright destructive of the church.

The Embarrassed Believer needs to remember that Peter, Christ's "rock," folded up like a cheap tent when he was accused of being a disciple of Jesus. Sure, it was a tough situation. Jesus had been dragged off and put on trial, the trial that would lead to His execution. And Peter had summoned up enough courage at least to follow his Lord to the buildings wherein the trial took place. But three times folks outside in the crowd challenged Peter to reveal himself as a follower of Jesus. And Peter flunked three times. Embarrassment and fear of identification as a Christian thus have a great pedigree.

In fact, the most inspiring Christian leaders I know are thoroughly sympathetic to the fears of the Embarrassed Believer and to the concerns of the unconverted seeker.

All genuine believers know how acutely discomforting the exploration of God can be. They have done the same thing, walked the same road. They are not dismissive of doubt's power.

If you want to know how hard it is to run a marathon, you do not ask the sedentary neighbor next door who watches a lot of ESPN. You find a marathon runner.

Bill and Julie Leach are friends of ours. Bill has competed in Hawaii's Ironman Triathlon, and Julie has actually won it. (In fact, Bill's the 1996 world champion triathlete in his age group.) They can describe with great detail how hard it actually is to complete the Ironman course. All others who haven't run the course are just guessing. If I ever needed to know some facts about a triathlon generally or the Ironman specifically, I'd ask Julie or Bill, not the scores of TV watchers who have glimpsed parts of one or more of these competitions.

That's exactly what seekers need to do. And it is especially what believers afraid of the world need to do. They need to ask folks who have been there at the gates of belief.

Of course, it's one thing to ask world-class athletes about their specialties. Faith is very different, because it's available to anyone, and there are thousands of people to ask about the particulars. The problem is in the asking. It could lead to embarrassment. Embarrassment is not a rare phenomenon. And anyone who has decided to seek God seriously runs into the embarrassment wall early on in the process. The sidelong glance, the half-smile, the shaking head—these are the marks of mirth. Greg Gagne, the Dodgers player profiled in the *Times* in early '96, was quoted as saying he knows the snickers and the scorn are constantly there, but he chooses to ignore them. That's not always easy, particularly for individuals either poised at faith's gates or just inside the walls.

What I have discovered in my conversations with individuals of deep faith is that it is indecision that carries vulnerability, not faith. It's the fear of profession of faith that tortures, not the actual profession. As with most other difficult choices, the hand-wringing is a far more painful process than the actual abuse that follows conversation or confession or both. Embarrassment at belief or even curiosity is thus largely self-inflicted.

Why? Because those who mock—and they are legion—generally turn out to be less-than-impressive intellects. Some, of course, are wildly successful, but not so successful as, say, Sir John Templeton, a confessing Christian who is the founder of the Templeton Prize. Intellectually, only a fool dismisses the possibility of God, and it is simply hard to feel embarrassment at the hands of a fool.

Let me put this another way. Embarrassment is the reaction to scorn. And who is likely to scorn religious belief? Not other orthodox believers, even from wildly different traditions. If my show taught me anything, it is the depth and genuineness of the respect with which religious *leaders* treat other traditions. Of course Christian leaders think Mormons and Muslims are widely wrong in their beliefs, and vice versa. But there is never scorn or mockery in their mutual critiques.

Nonbelievers are a different story, and my work in the media has allowed me to hear the uncensored contempt that media types hold for enthusiasts of all sorts. As I've said, detachment is as close to an unchallenged journalistic virtue as any that exists, and the sort of fierce emotional and intellectual loyalty displayed by religious folk is a fine target for media contempt.

But the key is that this contempt, real though it might be, is anti-intellectual and can proceed only from huge ignorance. I am fond of pointing out to nonbelievers that all their certainty is no match for Aquinas or Augustine. Some realize the trap and abandon the argument about the intellectual merits of faith. Others fall into the snare: "What do you expect from guys living hundreds of years ago?" The unstated premise of this reply is that the nonbeliever is on the side of Galileo and the believer is on the side of the Inquisition and the triumph of science has driven theology from the field.

This is a ludicrous claim advanced consciously or unconsciously by individuals of limited intellectual experience. Why? Because Aquinas, Augustine, and scores of other theologians do not argue with science at all. Like Homer, Socrates, Plato, Aristotle, Montaigne, Machiavelli, Locke, Hegel, and a hundred others, their ideas did not depend on Ptolemy's universe. People who think that Christian belief depends upon a limited grasp of natural science betray a huge learning gap as well as an intellectual sloth that ought to embarrass them. They are depending on the media and its accounts of such discredited academic exercises as the Jesus Seminar. Have they looked beyond the headlines? Doubtful.

I looked hard for excerpts from modern nonbelievers to include in the anthology for *Searching for God in America*. Mostly I settled for humorists like Mencken and Twain. I did cull some pages from John Dewey and William James, but their disbelief was of a distinctly unspirited kind. It turns out that Christian apologetics of the nineteenth and twentieth centuries may have lost the war by winning all the battles. I could find no compelling argument against faith to excerpt for any anthology. Faith had overwhelmed its opponents. The "triumph" of nonbelief was not a triumph at all. Instead it resulted from the proponents of nonbelief surrendering the field and refusing to fight. Darwin became an endpoint, not a beginning, and the opponents of belief took to intoning his name and closing off the conversation. And it worked.

Then the humorists took over—Twain and Mencken and their modern talk-show counterparts—and heckling replaced argument. Before long the subtle oppressions of embarrassment and silence had conquered the conversation.

But the intellectual debate was never lost by the proponents of belief. It's not my job, and it is beyond my abilities, to condense C. S. Lewis and Chesterton or to excerpt Aquinas and Augustine. I am not trained in apologetics. My point is more blunt: The folks who would embarrass you for having a faith must be comfortable debating and beating some of the greatest minds in history. The inspiration that comes from this recognition must be similar to that enjoyed by a close ally of the U.S.: You don't have to know anything about the U.S. military capability. You don't have to know how the U.S. would fight and win any conflict in which you might become involved. Rather, you are comfortable knowing that the U.S. would win if obliged to do so. Religious tradition is an arsenal for the believer even if he or she never even glimpses the inside of the fortress.

And you don't have to rely on ancients or even mid-century greats. The articulate and intellectually inspiring champions of belief are numerous. I think of the editor of *First Things* magazine Richard John Neuhaus, the Israeli Talmud scholar Adin Steinsaltz, and Berkeley Law School professor Philip Johnson, and I am immediately comforted that although I may be incredibly ill-equipped to argue my way out of any false dilemma posed by nonbelievers, there are plenty of scholars—indeed thousands—who easily could. Within driving distance of almost every American there is bound to be an articulate and earnest defender of the Christian faith.

The second comfort to those embarrassed by either the reality or the prospect of genuine belief is that the number of those hostile to faith is not so enormous as one might believe. The dominant media culture does hold up for praise a few thousand celebrities among whom it is difficult to find believers. The frustration I feel is that I *know* there are Christians among the celebrity caste who hold their faith close for fear of professional retribution. And the folks who define the media culture—elite print and electronic journalists—sometimes seem overwhelmingly hostile to traditional religion. But believers do themselves enormous harm by overestimating the pure numbers of their opponents and by underestimating how insecure these opponents are in their collective disbelief.

Sure, disparaging remarks are routine about "the religious right," and occasionally someone will take a public poke at Pat Robertson. But how often do you see a challenge thrown down at the feet of church leadership? In fact, political figures of all ideological stripes are eager to co-opt "mainstream" religious leaderships. Obvious attacks on belief are almost wholly absent from the culture. A recent survey of members of Congress revealed that all but two federal legislators declared themselves to be a Catholic, Protestant, or Jew. This reflects the underlying pattern of American self-description, and while the media do not often fairly reflect that pattern, the reality is undisturbed.

I have concluded that believers are overestimating the total strength of the hostility toward belief. Some certainly exists. But the desire for knowledge is much deeper and more widespread than is the contempt that will greet public manifestations of faith. In recent years, a few believers are becoming more and more bold about declaring and defending their faith. This kind of public embrace of faith is compelled by Christian belief. "I am not ashamed of the gospel," wrote Paul. As the fear of embarrassment drains away, the momentum of renewal will accelerate. But as some examples will illustrate, the renewal has a vast distance to travel before the overall culture begins to right itself again.

As I edited the final version of this book, Professor J. P. Moreland of Talbot School of Theology in Southern California sent me a copy of *Jesus under Fire,* the book he had coedited with Michael J. Wilkins, and the truth of the matter was driven home again. There in one place were some of the most powerful examples of modern apologetics, all organized completely and thoroughly to reply to the media darlings in the Jesus Seminar. The crushing rebukes delivered by *Jesus under Fire* have not received even 1 percent of the coverage accorded to the pink and red bead-throwers at the seminar. But a believer who reads, say, Craig Blomberg's essay "Where Do We Start Studying Jesus?" knows that "the Jesus Seminar and its friends do not reflect any consensus of scholars except for those on 'the radical fringe' of the field. Its methodology is seriously flawed and its conclusions unnecessarily skeptical." That a trained and careful scholar has provided the arguments and footnotes to support this conclusion is a great comfort.

Jesus under Fire is one of hundreds of new books that are but a small portion of all the resources available to the intellectually curious. Embarrassment is not a risk to those who will spend even a couple of days rummaging around the local library. The need to do so, the need to get past the embarrassment, is pressing, because the trajectory I referred to earlier has left the nonbelieving world with little to guide it.

F rom 1965 through 1974, I attended nearly every Cleveland Browns home game. They played in Cleveland's Municipal Stadium—a bulky monster of steel girders that could hold more than eighty thousand fans. I was there when Frank Ryan got booed off the field. I was there when Bill Nelson got booed off the field. I was there when Mike Phipps got booed off the field.

I was far away when Brian Sipe's unnecessary interception was thrown in 1980. I was far away for John Elway's ninety-nine-yard drive. I was far away for Earnest Byner's fumble (in Denver). All three of these events need no explanation for a Browns fan. This triple play of football disasters made me stronger as a Browns fan, not weaker. Even though I had moved and lived far away, even though I was often disappointed, I never flagged in my enthusiasm. On Sunday mornings I would leave after early church service and drive to a saloon to watch a satellite broadcast along with scores of other "Southern California Browns Backers"—the country's largest organization of sports fans not geographically contiguous to a team.

If my devotion were an illness, I could point to literally hundreds of thousands of similarly afflicted folks. It's a northern-eastern Ohio thing.

The routine of NFL game days from September to December in Cleveland had a talismanic quality right down to the stadium dogs and mustard. In the years prior to 1995, the Dawg Pound got a lot of attention, but Browns fans were many, many thousands more, and more intense than the fellows with the masks.

Some folks argue that other sports franchises have a more loyal following than did the Browns—the Celtics, the Bruins, and the Red Sox are offered up, and of course, the Cubs. But until you've sat through a few Lake Erie chill factors, I don't call it dedicated.

In 1995 the owner of the Browns decided he wanted to make more money. He'd badly mismanaged the team, and his net worth had declined. The soup kitchen didn't beckon, but creditors did. He could have done the honorable thing and sold the team and kept a small interest, but this owner's ego has always been far larger than his talent, so he couldn't just sell. Rather, contrary to any normal idea of honor—and indifferent to any quaint idea of "the common good"—the owner breached a verbal agreement with the fans, opened negotiations with Baltimore, and concluded a secret deal to spirit the NFL's most beloved franchise out of town. That he broke millions of hearts did not deter him in the least.

I remind readers of this bit of perfidy because it illustrates the problem the rest of this book deals with. As we approach the new millennium, it is fair to say that the idea of an agreed-upon public morality is absurd in the minds of many. How can anyone expect even a substantial minority of Americans to believe in an accepted code of morality when every day's paper showcases the tattered state of ethics of public people? If, to use my example, the owner of the Browns is free to break an unwritten but real compact with millions of people and to do so in the face of withering criticism from some of his fellow franchise owners—in short, if power is all that matters—then how can a reasonable person appeal to moral standards?

I have picked this example not only because this sorry episode occurred during the year I was making *Searching for God in America* but also because it was such a transparently bad thing for the owner to do—so utterly base an act. And yet, it happened. People with the power to stop it—other NFL owners—did not. So who's going to argue about "universal moral standards"?

There is only one response: We know the Browns' owner was wrong to do what he did. Everyone in Cleveland knows this. Everyone who follows football knows this. The commissioner knows this. The people of Baltimore know this.

In fact, Art Modell knows this. He knows he did a very, very bad thing, an act of betrayal so obvious that he's guaranteed himself a level of infamy reserved usually for felons. Modell had the power to accomplish his dishonorable end but not the authority to cover it in even a thin robe of respectability.

Because outrage is still possible over public acts of dishonor, it means that there still exist some common conventions of morality. There is still some ability to appeal to shared notions of right and wrong. Granted, it's a diminished core, and it's getting smaller all the time. But it's still there. And that which remains should be preserved.

In the time since *Searching for God in America* first aired, I have been asked to address audiences of extraordinary variety on the subject of spirituality in America. Those invitations underscore the ongoing renewal of belief in America that I mentioned two chapters back. Those who are participating in these forums come equipped with some common moral understandings. Even after thirty years of relentless relativism, there still endures some bedrock agreement about what is right and what is wrong. The collapse is not complete. It is ongoing, but it is not complete.

That bedrock provides the foundation on which to rebuild a broader moral consensus. So much of "conventional" morality has been abandoned in the past thirty years that the scaffolding is going to be up for a long time. But at least we know that some common ground remains around which moral community can organize.

And for that recognition we can thank Art Modell. Even the most painfully self-conscious Christian must recognize that God's created order may be ignored by the larger culture, and those who proclaim it may be mocked, but still that natural order remains. Whenever common acclamation or revulsion sweeps the general public, chances are that the culture has collided again in an unavoidable way with moral absolutes. When those collisions occur, believers should be pushed to proclaim the real significance of moral agreement—that there is such a thing! Once proclaimed, the obvious question must be addressed— where did it come from, this moral agreement? And believers should have the answer.

Who Is the Embarrassed Believer, and What Does He or She Need to Do?

Before we turn to the job of the Christian in modern America, the term "Embarrassed Believer" deserves a touch more explanation.

By now it is apparent that I believe EBs to number in the tens of millions. In fact, I suspect that they are in the majority in most congregations in the U.S. and probably the world.

That's a pretty bold assertion. And I make it without benefit of polling data, a statistically significant survey sample, or academic support. It's just true. In fact, it's got to be true.

We know that oxygen is present in the air by virtue of the fact that people are breathing. Withdraw the oxygen, and folks will quickly begin to collapse left and right. Though oxygen cannot be seen, counted, or in any way measured by laymen, laymen are certainly in a position to judge whether oxygen is present.

Christians of the un-embarrassed sort are pretty easy to spot. Laymen can pick 'em out. No authoritative list of the "ten warning signs of a Christian" has been published, but it wouldn't be that hard to devise.

I am not referring to professional Christians. Professional Christians are those who make their living by virtue of their Christian ministry. It is a noble and wonderful calling to be a professional Christian; in fact it may be the highest calling. But EBs are almost exclusively amateur Christians; that is, they have jobs and lives not necessarily connected to the church.

We know that the number of amateur Christians who are EBs is legion, because we see the effects of their absence from the larger culture just as vividly as we would see the effects of the withdrawal of oxygen from a crowded room.

Look. More than fifty million men, women, and children who attend Christian church on a very regular basis. That's a very, very low estimate; and I use this purposefully understated number to emphasize the truth of the argument. If even half of this low number were not Embarrassed Believers, then there would be twenty-five million *bold* Christians wandering around the country.

Do you see the evidence of twenty-five million bold Christians at work in the U.S. in 1998? Of course not! The counterargument is implausible. The country could not be—literally, *could not be*—in the condition it is in if there were that many bold Christians wandering around.

Let me put it another way. If there were 2.5 million bold Christians in California, do you suppose the entertainment industry would be the way it is? The movie industry? The record industry? Of course not.

Now let me argue the stronger case. In poll after poll, 90 percent of Americans state that they believe in God. Whenever I see some version of that statistic, I'm forced to ask, What kind of God? Given the pathetic level of evidence of genuine belief in God, it must be a God that doesn't much care whether or not His people take notice of Him.

Certainly I'm no shining example of boldness. My "public" profession of belief dates to my thirty-fifth year, when the subject came up on my radio show. Sure, my family and my friends knew that I attended church, but who knows how many of them thought of that faith as a significant part of my life?

If the men and women at your place of work or at your child's school were to be asked, "Does so-and-so believe in God?" what would their answer be?

Let me put this another, more concrete way. In the spring of 1985, I went to work in the U.S. Department of Justice as a Special Assistant to the Attorney General. That job required that I receive a security clearance. A year later I went to work in the White House Counsel's Office, and a couple of years after that I was nominated for and eventually confirmed by the U.S. Senate for a pretty high-up job in one of the capital's endless alphabet agencies. At each of those points, the FBI conducted one level or another of a field investigation. Agents would call or visit old friends and neighbors, as well as my parents' friends and neighbors, to ask questions about me, my past, and my fitness to handle national security information. The reports of these interviews were packaged into a folder and provided for the inspection of various folks. Tens of thousands of these background checks are done every year.

I never saw my own file, but I'm curious whether any mention of my Christian faith made it into those reports. In my capacity as a White House lawyer, I read quite a few of these reports prepared on other people, and I do not recall many references to religious beliefs. In fact, I don't recall any.

The conclusion I reach is that religious belief, especially for orthodox Christians, is a highly compartmentalized part of their lives. Clearly there are nominal Christians who are that in name only, who attend church or declare themselves to be believers by force of habit. But the greater number seem to me to be EBs. These are folks who really do believe. They believe fervently, in fact, and they pray. But they do so within the compartment of their life given over to God.

The easiest test concerns the Bible. How many believers have Bibles on their desks or near their work stations or somewhere within range of their work routine, be it a locker, a cupboard, or even the car they drive to and from in? Bibles are ubiquitous in the lives of the model Christians I've known. These books are everywhere (the goofiest translations, too, I might add, but a Bible nevertheless)! Some may object that this is a relatively unsophisticated test of the boldness of the believer in question, but how bold can a believer be if he or she is physically separated from Scripture?

Ratchet up the test: How many believers host a small group for prayer or Bible study in their home or at work? That sort of commitment is unthinkable to millions of believers. It involves the display of faith in a setting where . . . well, where what? Well, where the believer would run the risk of some sort of penalty, real or imagined. In most cases the penalty would be, at worst, a few snide comments or some gentle poking of fun for being a Holy Roller. There might be more serious repercussions, but I've heard of only a few cases. Discrimination on the basis of religious belief is illegal, but most folks know that most mockery is not of the actionable sort.

Most EBs don't push against these walls, these conventions of behavior, when it comes to expressions of faith, even those as simple as the availability of Scripture. Some do. They have blown past the fear of embarrassment. But if you are not among them, you need to understand why the change to boldness is necessary, why it is in fact crucial.

It's about changing lives. EB are believers. They have faith. They have salvation, in fact. And as their lives are sanctified, they have greater and greater measures of genuine joy. Their embarrassment in the world does not cut them off from Christ.

No, the problem is that the world is cut off from the believer in his or her full power.

Here's a really horrible sports analogy. If Michael Jordan were limited to one end of the court, he'd still be the best player on that court. But he wouldn't be the most crucial player to the game's outcome, because he'd have only a limited range within which to showcase his skills. And even if he scored an all-time high in such a game, his satisfaction could not be equal to that which would have accompanied a complete game. And certainly his coach, Phil Jackson, would not be pleased.

Embarrassed believers need to defeat their reticence for three reasons. First, the world needs fully formed and committed Christians. An underground of Christians is better than no Christians at all, but it accomplishes the equivalent of the French underground in World War II—much good, in other words, but not nearly enough.

Second, the believer needs to live the fully exposed Christian life because it moves the believer, to use C. S. Lewis's phrase from the last book in *The Chronicles of Narnia,* "further up and further in." The fully devoted Christian cannot lead a compartmentalized life, which is another way of saying that the Sunday experience of God needs to become a seven-day-a-week experience of God.

Finally, the EB needs to become an ex-EB because God commands it. Search Scripture for an example of a once-a-week Christian. Write me when you find him or her.

If you have seen yourself in the preceding pages, let me assure you that you have seen me as well. I am a credentialed EB who's been changing over the past five years. I backed into my public Christianity reluctantly. I was and am a secular journalist. The radio talk show that launched my television career was a secular radio show. But because I found myself surrounded by very bold Christians, and because their example humbled me, I eventually made a timid step or two toward public discussion of my faith.

When the idea came to me to feature a few religious guests on my program, it led to reading C. S. Lewis's *Mere Christianity* over the air. And that led to *Searching for God in America*. And that led to this book. That sequence has led me to the most significant observation I've noticed in the past half-decade: The most joyful Christians are those who do not worry a bit about what the world thinks but who concern themselves continually with what God thinks. That approach, I assure you, leaves little room for embarrassment.

But even if embarrassment drops away, there is still a great risk. Fear of personal embarrassment is an obstacle. But fear of embarrassing the church is a great caution. Here's a blunt warning: You can do a lot more harm than good by bold professions of Christian belief at the wrong time, in the wrong place, or in the wrong manner.

And that's the tension. We are called to witness for Christ, but we are warned not to call the church into public disgrace. There is a way to do both. And it requires both some work, and a whole bunch of community.

HELLO, I MUST BE GOING

I had been "bumped" from the *Today Show Sunday.* And in a most unceremonious way. The network had sent a car to gather me up at 6:30 A.M., and I strode confidently into the greenroom at Rockefeller Center only to be met by the booker and the senior producer. "Hi," said the latter. "I'm sorry, but Shimon Peres is here, and I can't use you. I hope you understand."

Since I host a nightly news and public affairs show in the Los Angeles market, I could hardly object that I'd flown three thousand miles for the interview. The rules were well known to me: There is no such thing as a "sure thing" interview until the broadcast is over. So I actually smiled and wandered off in an orderly way. A car was offered. I declined and walked back to the hotel.

There I met my friend Richard Bryant for breakfast. A large-hearted man with an ever-present smile, Richard immediately viewed the morning's nonevent in an unusual way: "You have certainly made it when it takes Shimon Peres to knock you off the *Today Show.*" We chuckled. We ate.

And I was glad to have traveled cross-country, because I spent a beautiful July Sunday in the company of a great friend who had only recently left the West Coast for the East Coast. We enjoyed breakfast. We visited the Museum of Modern Art and took in a much-reviewed Picasso exhibit. We surveyed New York from the top of the Empire State Building, and we walked a not too crowded but still very vibrant midtown.

And we went to church.

The Fifth Avenue Presbyterian Church is a magnificent old building on the corner of Fifth Avenue and Fifty-Fifth Street. We learned that it is not an air-conditioned church and that hand-fans are still a part of services at this particular tall-steeple church.

I had once heard a talk by Fifth Avenue's senior pastor, Dr. Thomas K. Tewell, and had hoped to find him in the pulpit that Sunday. But of course, he knew about the fans and New York City in July and was on vacation. Dr. Bernard Johnson, the senior pastor of Hope Church, Richfield, Minnesota, was the guest preacher that day. I still wonder whether he had been alerted to the absence of air conditioning before he agreed to the visit. The sermon title, "Lo, I Am with You Always" telegraphed his intent to expand on Matthew 28:19–20, in which Christ instructed His disciples: "Go therefore and make disciples of all nations, baptizing them in the name of the Father and of the Son and of the Holy Spirit, teaching them to observe all that I have commanded you; and lo, I am with you always, to the close of the age."

Dr. Johnson delivered a magnificent message, made even more powerful by the fact that he abbreviated it in response to the soaring temperature inside the sanctuary.

What the preacher conveyed to the congregation was the image of Groucho Marx in a standard routine of his: "Hello," Marx would say. "I must be going." The juxtaposition of the greeting with the exit line was funny when Marx said it. It's still funny today.

What's not funny at all, Dr. Johnson pointed out, was how that phrase—Hello, I must be going— has come to describe most human relationships as this millennium comes to a close.

Millions of marriages—Hello, I must be going.

Children and parents—Hello, I must be going.

Professional colleagues and coworkers—Hello, I must be going.

Church members, leaders, and pastors—Hello, I must be going.

Just plain old friends—Hello, I must be going.

What Dr. Johnson was underscoring was the crumbling of civic cement. The relationships that not so long ago defined and bordered a life have begun dissolving on a massive scale.

A. T. Rohl was my grandfather. When he died at 101 in 1993, he had lived a full century in the same town, Ashtabula, Ohio. He'd been a member of the fire department for more than fifty years. A.T. had perhaps traveled to Pennsylvania and Indiana, though I'm not sure that he ever left the great state of his birth. A Catholic, he had probably attended Mass five thousand times in the same church. "Hello, I must be going" was not part of A.T.'s life.

My wife's grandmother was slightly more mobile, having married into the navy. She lived where officers' wives lived—a variety of posts around the world. But she died in an apartment on Connecticut Avenue in Washington, D.C., where she had been living for more than forty years.

My parents, to whom this book is dedicated, celebrated their fiftieth anniversary in the summer of 1996. They've lived in Warren, Ohio, since 1949. Dad's still practicing with the same law firm he joined that year. They owned three different houses in that stretch, and their friends have been their friends for nearly half a century. During the last few weeks of my mother's life in the fall of 1997, she was visited by and received encouragement from a circle of friends and family that had surrounded her for forty years or more.

My wife and I have had a dozen addresses in six cities spread over two states and the District of Columbia. We've been married fifteen years and plan on staying that way. But we are clearly living very differently from our parents and their parents. I've had ten different full-time jobs since graduating from college in 1978 and have been happy with each of them and happy as well to greet a new challenge when it came along. My Christmas card list, which I try to limit to significant people from our past who are now separated by geography, is a catalog of good-byes—none of which were easy to bid. "Hello, I must be going" is a pretty good label for the Hewitts.

The fragmenting of community implicit in the rise of "Hello, I must be going" lifestyles has left hundreds of thousands, indeed millions, of people more or less defenseless against the sometimes sudden, sometimes terrible shocks of life. When illness arises in a heretofore healthy young adult, when a learning disability is diagnosed in a young child, when a teen uses drugs, when an older parent develops Alzheimer's, when a middle-ager loses a job . . . At these moments community is necessary as a buffer, a semi-shock absorber.

In the "Hello, I must be going" era, the transience of individuals has shorn away many protective layers.

If only out of self-interest, the church in America ought to be growing by dramatic increases in membership. Any church in any community ought to be a quick entry point for new arrivals in town or even the newly insecure or hurting. The congregation with open arms is—regardless of theology—a refuge.

But the numbers haven't been growing even as millions have expressly undertaken searches for God or meaning. It seems an inescapable conclusion that many, many churches are not in the welcoming mode; they are either not committed to providing refuge and community, or they are clueless about how to put out the welcome mat.

Perhaps overload is the reason. Even the most receptive of church congregations can be overmatched by a rising tide of tragedy and loneliness; the volume of which staggers the objective observer. There are so many tales of misfortune and loss on every cul-de-sac that it may be unreasonable to expect any institution to be ready to meet the need.

But if, as I have seen in some places, churches become scrums of the well-off and the well-adjusted, huddled together against what is literally one hell of a storm outside, those churches will have failed their central mission.

In an era of "Hello, I must be going," the church must stand opposite that trend with an earnest invitation to enter and to stay, and not just for a while but for as many years as God wills life to exist.

There are signs. Listen for a bit to any Christian radio station. A community-events schedule including a dozen or more openings into the Christian community will be broadcast. Other faiths as well have taken to the religion pages to advertise their inclusiveness and their times of gathering. Clearly, some congregations are attempting to open themselves.

Good things, certainly. But the critical need is for the hundred million Americans who attended some sort of church, synagogue, or mosque in the past fortnight to become part of the ingathering of the dispersed American people. One of the great fears of those who do not belong to *any* community is that *no* community will welcome them. It is not an irrational fear.

The believers, confident of where they belong and with whom they stand, may find this startling. Are there not greeters? Isn't the sign of peace passed? Aren't the Sunday morning smiles contagious?

They are. But they are not enough. The Embarrassed Believer, especially, needs to find a church home that is eager to support his or her faith.

Rick Warren is the pastor of Saddleback Valley Community Church in Orange County, California. Rick's church now averages more than twelve thousand in weekly attendance and has thirty-four thousand members on its rolls. It did not exist until he began knocking on doors in 1980. Obviously he has found a design that works. How does he teach his congregation to welcome?

Rick emphasized to me that Saddleback Valley Community Church is a *family*—not an institution—an ethic he labors to instill in every member. Yes, there are trained greeters positioned and eager to welcome new faces, and there is a thorough strategy of inclusion that permeates every program the church provides. "Some people may think you're shallow because you're strategic," Rick warned, "but we are purpose-driven, and that purpose has to be strategically executed." More than 80 percent of Rick's members had no religious affiliation for years prior to passing through his doors. His staff, his preaching, and his congregation have as their mission the embrace and inclusion of the unchurched.

It works for Rick Warren and his community, and it can work everywhere. One deep need is for believers to risk the embarrassment and extend an invitation to others to come along to a service—to check out the "family," as Rick called it. Indeed, one of the most extraordinary steps a believer can take is to invite an outsider to an extended time of fellowship—a retreat or a weekend fellowship. The crucial ingredient is accompaniment of a newcomer into a strange place.

The guy in the next office, the mom or dad in the school carpool, the teller at the bank with whom you have exchanged common courtesies for a couple of years—each may be waiting for a welcome into a community of faith. In fact, their lives may depend on it; their eternal lives may depend on it. The antithesis of "Hello, I must be going," is "Would you like to come along?" It is an antidote for the alienation of the modern world, and every believer can prescribe it.

And before you declare yourself or your neighbor as "not the joiner type," consider who is. There are a thousand excuses to avoid the kind of commitment that deep church involvement demands or the kind of embarrassment that a rejected invitation summons up. But as the most successful people in the secular world recognize the need for community, surely Christians can do so as well.

The Young Presidents Organization is a club for very successful and relatively young people. Membership is limited to presidents or chief executive officers of substantial companies who have achieved that rank prior to the age of forty. When you hit fifty you get bounced, although alums are treated with the dignity that typically attends old friends with net worth in seven figures.

In the past few years, I've been asked to speak to various YPO chapters throughout Southern California. I always accept and juggle the schedule to accommodate the requests.

I speak to the groups for a few reasons. First, my former boss Richard Nixon used to speak to them and did so because he understood that business owners and operators are individuals of unique, if somewhat muted, influence in their communities. Inevitably it is successful businesspeople who power much of the private sector's charitable and philanthropic efforts, and these efforts deserve some reciprocity from political conservatives like me who are always lecturing the private sector on its responsibilities.

There is also among its members a sense of confidence and achievement that I enjoy. Very successful businesspeople come equipped with a confidence that is mirrored by people of great faith and by world-class athletes. Such an attitude is contagious.

Finally, I welcome the chance to observe horizontal elites at play. Now there's a mouthful of sociology for you, but it's a fairly easy concept to understand.

Elites are, of course, groups of successful people; and while the categories of achievement can change—business, law, the arts, academia—when they organize themselves into clubs, the interactions are immediately revealing.

First, YPOs need community as much as anyone, but their success limits their opportunity for community. It's not that they are snobby, and they certainly are not shy. But the demands of running a business are extraordinary. Because YPO membership is accompanied by a commitment and a very well-developed scheduling apparatus, these people find in YPO a ready-made refuge—a club of equals who share the common problems of running a business of a certain size and who meet at regular and predictable intervals. Membership is not about preening or display but about friendship. Probably the most frequent comment I have heard from YPOs is that they value their "forums" with an almost scary ferocity. "Forums" are simply small groups of YPOs that meet regularly over long periods of time and thus develop trust and a deep sense of friendship among forum members.

It is this dynamic that I find so attractive. Even these very successful and generally very well adjusted folks hunger for deep friendship. The YPO group facilitates those friendships. That's the entire reason for the organization's existence. The club sponsors good lectures and programs, certainly; and its "universities" are unique opportunities to combine learning and leisure and travel. But, at its core, it's about friendship.

This desire is not unique to very successful business owners. It is a universal impulse, a need so inbred that I have never known a single person who could not, with a couple of moments' reflection, name his or her closest friends over the course of his or her life, whether long or short.

Friends are the face of God in everyday life. They are the expression of complete love and acceptance, and yet a challenge to do better.

As the "Hello, I must be going" society has emerged, the possibilities of genuine friendship have narrowed. Genuine friendship requires a rough proportionality of natural talents and tastes as well as the opportunity that only time allows for acquaintance to mature into friendship.

Among the renewing aspects of the church in America is its recognition of this need for friendship. Among those churches experiencing explosive growth there is a near-uniform emphasis on small-group ministry. Like the YPO "forums," this small-group device is an instrument that facilitates friendships that have grown up in a world unforgiving in its demands on time and stability.

Christian friendship brings with it a special quality that not even the closest friendships among nonbelievers can approximate. For within the shared experience of Christ is a purposefulness and joy that enriches every aspect of a friendship. And the notion of accountability as well becomes much more pervasive.

Accountability is a catchword within the small-group movement in the church and in a variety of other settings as well. I cannot be certain, but I suspect that accountability is a watchword of YPO forums, as well as within leadership training seminars and Twelve Step programs.

Accountability means simply the openness to correction: the willingness to be called upon to account for action or inaction. The setting within which accountability occurs is indicative of the expansiveness of the accountability.

Accountability within a bridge club might mean as little as showing up and playing by the rules (except via the standard "conventions"—a wonderful bridge term I can only understand as a polite expression for cheating).

Accountability among business partners might mean living up to the express or implied agreement of level of effort or division of profit.

Accountability within a church membership can mean something as casual as attendance. Certainly it does not necessarily mean a level of giving or a level of commitment of time. In fact, in most churches there's very little in the way of accountability. If you belong to a church, ask yourself, are you accountable for any particular duty or level of participation?

One of the attractions of the YPO meetings I've attended is the sharp air of accountability. Rotarians will know—I've spoken to dozens of these groups as well—that at their gatherings a series of small fines is assessed against late arrivers, early leavers, and meeting missers. That's a fun kind of accountability that raises dollars for charity. YPOs approach their membership obligations with a much more serious air. The "day chair" for a YPO event—the individual accountable to the chapter for the success or failure of a particular program—will nearly drive a lecturer like me crazy with pre-event planning. No number of assurances as to my on-time habits or past experiences will typically suffice. Day chairs do not want to let their colleagues down, so they hector the speakers. Accountability brings such attention to detail.

Belief that is new requires some support. Belief that is old can use some energy. Belief that is embarrassed can use a kick in the pants. The transmission of belief to the unchurched and the defense of belief to the hostile requires not individuals of great talent but groups of individuals of collective great talent. YPOs are not slackers. They are, in fact, a definition of a certain measure of success.

Those who would defend belief and advance it have to ask themselves, "If some group accountability works for YPOs, ought it to work for me as well?" What holds back far too many believers from membership in such a group is—by now you should know this answer—a fear of embarrassment. We are dealing with a generation of Christians who know better than to expose their faith and their fears to public ridicule. And we are positively wired to put distance between ourselves and any kind of enthusiasm that smells of fanaticism. Even Christians of unquestioned conversion have explained to me that small-group Bible study or simply fellowship is an exercise they'd just as soon bypass.

Some argue it's a fear of intimacy, and perhaps it is. But substitute "friendship" for "intimacy," and you have a nonsense notion that some people don't want friends.

Here's a thought. A faith-based small group meets for a reason. It is called into being because of the promptings of the Holy Spirit to seek a deeper knowledge of God. It may be that reluctant joiners are not afraid of what they won't find but rather of what they will—a very real sense of God's call on their lives.

You Can Test for Authenticity

I n this chapter, I must pause to denounce myself. Bear with me. There is not an airport bookstore in America that does not overflow with instant-inspiration books. Folks about to board airplanes obviously reach for Ludlum, Grisham, or enlightenment. The mass-market novelists have not been displaced, but they are now in the company of hundreds of titles aimed at inspiration.

This genre has its superstars: Scott Peck, Stephen Covey, and early on in this book I mentioned Fulghum, Bly, and Redfield. I aspire to join them. I want that shelf space for this book. I will be pleased to crack the bestseller list.

So the general denunciation of all such books has got to include me.

Friends, you can't get "there" from "here." You can't get there in the company of Steven Covey. You can't get there in the company of Scott Peck. And you most definitely cannot get there in the company of James Redfield. Maybe I will save you some wrong turns and point you in the right direction, but you can't get there with me either.

Where is "there"?

"There" is belief in and relationship with God. Period. "There" is not inner peace or contentment or significance or success or happiness. The only destination that makes sense is God, and the only book that's critical is Scripture. And nothing else will get you there.

So, should you lay this book down? That depends on what you will pick up in its place. This book is preferable to millions of others and less preferable than some. It's unlikely that you have any of the others close at hand, so stick with this one for a while. Other titles are sprinkled throughout. Make a list.

The instant-inspiration industry has sprung up because of the awful emptiness of American life for those not in relationship with God. The industry is a substitute for that relationship. It doesn't work for long, which explains why the industry is busy churning out dozens of new titles every month. "Less filling, tastes great" is more than a beer slogan; it's a label for this industry.

A year ago I was called upon to address a breakfast group of Christian businessmen, and I began by stating that the one hundred or so men had come for one of two things—the fellowship or the jolt.

The fellowship idea is the concept of a friendship not yet matured— that in a room of people drawn to an event like this there would be many friendly faces, and among them possibly a future true friend. Many had come for the chance to find a good friend. But many had come for a jolt.

A jolt is any message that hits us where we are, that breaks through our indifference and our suspicion. When we encounter a jolt—in a movie, a song, a sermon—we are dazzled and moved. So little of what we experience is profound, that our appetite for the profound is huge and always growing. We long for jolts.

Friends give us comfort and joy, but jolts give us truth and wisdom. The inspiration industry promises jolts but delivers feeble little sparks, like the tiny shocks of static electricity that build up when shuffling across carpet. But without a connection to God, these tiny shocks are better than nothing at all, and the industry provides a steady stream of them.

Much of what is produced by the instant-inspiration industry is silly, goofy really, and treated with a wholly undeserved respect. I do not need to name particular books or authors. A simple test will suffice to separate the genuine from the false.

Does a book tell you that God will ask hard things of you? That God will demand real sacrifice? That faith is hard? That the good life is hard? That from the easy stuff—the giving away of money—to the hard stuff—the giving away of life—God constantly demands more and more until eventually all is given over?

The more that is demanded and the less that is promised, in terms of comfort and wealth, the greater the likelihood that the book in question is authentically God-centered.

Embarrassed believers ought to consider this truth carefully. Courage is required of genuine Christians, and courage is an admirable quality. Sacrifice is demanded of genuine Christians, and self-sacrifice is usually applauded, at least by people whose applause matters to us. Believers are thus engaged in a life that is admirable and praiseworthy, so embarrassment is out of place. And, I think, most Christians know this. They know they ought not to be embarrassed, and they know that mockery ought not to dissuade them. Still they are chagrined. Yet the strangest ideas are publicly embraced and defended by the purveyors of New Age silliness without so much as a backward glance, even though no genuine courage or sacrifice is involved in their practice.

Why, then, the reticence among Christians and the boldness among the New Age set? Because New Age silliness is guaranteed a free ride in the media and the public. No matter how goofy, a respectful silence will be maintained unless the belief system is orthodox Christianity. If it is orthodox Christianity, demands for answers will be made.

Have you ever heard a hard-core New Age representative like Redfield or Deepak Chopra put on the firing line? I haven't. Interviewed, yes. But grilled? Never. Occasionally an article will appear that targets the snappy promises of New Age—Chopra was the subject, for example, of a scathing cover story in the *Weekly Standard.* But a respectful silence greets even the most poorly written treatise of nonsense like Redfield's *The Tenth Insight.* Even when I interviewed him, I extended the courtesy of a host to a guest and did not denounce him but merely led him instead into making rather ridiculous statements.

Contrast the free pass extended to New Age or "Eastern" thinkers with the reception extended to traditional Christianity. Nearly every bold Christian will find himself or herself pressed for answers to questions that have haunted theologians for centuries: Why is there suffering? Why do good people lose out to bad people? What happens to remote peoples who never hear the gospel? The game of "Stump the Christian" has been around for two millennia. Nonbelievers love it and do not hesitate to challenge the orthodox even if they would never dream of asking a Buddhist for evidence of karma.

And that's a large part of the explanation for the embarrassment that dogs many Christians. Many, many Christians don't have the answers to the questions posed in the game of "Stump the Christian." The answers exist. They have been developed by the greatest minds in human history. God has revealed Himself in Scripture, and great apologists from Paul forward have argued the case for Christ. But unless those answers are known, they are of no help.

Which is why the dumbing down of Christian belief has produced Embarrassed Believers by the millions.

N ow we approach the "how-to" section of this book. Until now I've been arguing the need for Christian belief and the consequences of its absence. Now we begin to grapple with the mechanics of defending belief. I start with one of the common denominators of American life, *Gilligan's Island.*

Gilligan's Island featured a core cast familiar to millions of Americans: Gilligan, the hopeless, lazy, but large-souled hero. Skipper, the big, blustery, lovable bear of a captain. The Howells, wealthy beyond belief. Movie star Ginger. Plain-and-simple Mary Ann. And, of course, the Professor.

Richard Bryant, the communications guru for the New Jersey Center for the Performing Arts, taught me to use these characters to recall the seven deadly sins:

Gilligan—sloth
Skipper—gluttony
Mr. Howell—anger
Mrs. Howell—greed
Ginger—lust
Mary Ann—envy
The Professor—pride

While it's a stretch to attribute envy to Mary Ann and pride to the Professor—both of whom serve as the castaway saints in residence—the device works.

I used it in the summer of 1996 to teach the seven deadly sins to a class of ten- and eleven-year-olds. It's a teacher's trick. I use teacher's tricks with law school classes as well. Information in the '90s needs some kind of intellectual Velcro if it's going to catch and hold.

The rush of information—the constant torrential downpour of facts, opinion, sound, and fury—makes teaching a much more difficult process than it used to be. There was a time when the only book in a house was the Bible and the only diversion from work was that one book. As families accumulated books, they were of a didactic sort—*The Pilgrim's Progress,* the McGuffy *Readers,* and similar standards. As printing became cheaper, newspapers and magazines began to show up, but it's a safe bet that the turn-of-the century household received information from no more than a half-dozen sources, at least one of which would almost universally be Scripture.

That world got blown to bits with the arrival of radio, with its numerous stations, and it's seen exponential growth in information ever since.

The pulpit competes for the attention of the pew-sitters with literally thousands of choices. Getting people into a church is itself a major achievement. Getting them, and their children, to remember anything for an hour or so is also a success worthy of praise. How teachers in classrooms do it amazes me.

Even the language presents an obstacle because it's so dumbed down. To teach requires common language. In addition to the greatest-hits list of sins, I have tried to teach the essentials of the great virtues. Try explaining *fortitude* to near-adolescents. Luckily, one of my colleagues, Keith, offered up the word *guts* as a synonym, and we had another grappling hook into their heads.

Over the ten-week summer session, we repeated the seven sins and seven virtues (in addition to fortitude, they are faith, hope, charity, justice, prudence, and temperance) often enough that a few of these young folks should have stowed it permanently. And the outline of church history we reviewed each week may also end up in a more-or-less fixed place in a few minds; though all I really hope for is that the idea that the church does have a history—a fixed, objectively true history—will find some adhesive somewhere. Modest goals for a teacher, I admit, but we are all working against that huge tide I touched on. To switch metaphors, we were trying that summer to be heard over the din of *Independence Day, The Rock,* and *The Blowfish.* That's tricky. Thus, *Gilligan's Island.*

And that's why one of the country's preeminent evangelists, Greg

Laurie of the Harvest Crusades, uses stories from *People* magazine and lyrics from Sting's most recent album to illustrate his sermons and whatever else he can lay his hands on that works. He's using the culture to break through the culture in order to teach the essentials of the gospel. As a result, on July 4, 1996, he preached to sixty-three thousand people in Anaheim Stadium. I'd say he's got the teaching method down.

Now that method must spread. While the United States and the West generally have achieved a level of material wealth simply unimaginable fifty years ago, its soul is diseased. Pick your own statistic—violent deaths, school test scores, one-parent families, profits for the pornography industry, heroin addiction. It's that trajectory problem again. All of these indicators point to the conclusion of spiritual disease. Christians don't just have an answer. They have *the* answer. But what must occur is the modern equivalent of Luther's translation of the Bible into German.

When Luther took up his pen and translated the Scriptures into the language of his people, he was replicating the great theologian Tertullian's triumph of the late second and early third century—taking the gospel from a difficult place to an accessible place. Tertullian wrote in Latin, the language of the people, putting aside Greek, the language of the elite. Luther threw Latin overboard for German, the language of his people. The principle of accessibility was thus the powerful engine of the Reformation.

Now the church must remake itself again. Not through political power, but through the culture. The church is producing its own culture, its own means of production beyond the pulpit. Some decry the birth of a Christian music industry because of the greed of some and the clay feet of others. No doubt they exist, just as false leaders of the gospel existed in Paul's day.

But that the accessibility process will result in some miscues does not—*cannot*—mean it ought to be abandoned. The church must use any and all means available to hold up the gospel. Later in this book, I'll talk about the danger in building up a parallel, Christian culture, but the lesson I've seen played out over and over again is that faith needs to be communicated with the audience in mind. And the modern audience arrives at the task with a diminished attention span and very little patience for books. The most persuasive defense of faith will matter not a whit if it's never heard.

Embarrassed believers have collectively lost their voice— their witness to the world in which they live—of a good news that transcends and transforms everyday life. Even if embarrassment at being thought slightly or greatly loony or out of touch can be overcome, then conviction to witness will have to be accompanied by new techniques of communicating the gospel. Luther needed German; Luthers of the twenty-first century will need all of the techno-terms and immersion in the popular culture they can endure.

But once you are heard, be prepared for the good . . . and the unusual.

A ritual has sprung up in recent years concerning the release of new books. Stores seek out authors to come and greet the public and autograph the books. What had once been an event limited to a few "major" bookstores is now routine in every bookseller's shop. Stores do more than invite; in fact, they push hard for certain authors. That's easy enough to understand. If you can coax my former colleague at L.A.'s KFI radio, Dr. Laura Schlesinger, into your store, then the crowd to buy a book will wind around the parking lot, patiently waiting in line to meet and greet her.

Some authors ask stores for a chance to hold an event in the hope that a "signing" will bring increased attention to their books. Bookstores, though, are not in a hurry to host authors who do not have a demonstrated record of attracting shoppers.

When *Searching for God in America* was published in the early summer of 1996, my presence was requested at a number of stores. My work as a broadcast journalist had long ago taught me that extended contact with the public can be wearying and a little alarming, even for minor celebrities like me. Far too many people confuse regular appearances on television with genuine influence, and some look forward to the chance to harangue a broadcaster in person.

But my home station, KCET-TV in Los Angeles, is one of the pioneers in the PBS network when it comes to weaning the station from its dependence on federal largess. One crucial step in that effort was to open, in partnership with some experienced retailers, a series of retail stores that sell PBS-connected videos, books, and a variety of educational toys and games. They are called "Stores of Knowledge," and they are found all around Southern California and will soon be throughout the U.S.

When the station's liaison with the stores asked me to make a half-dozen ninety-minute appearances to sign books and greet customers at some of the Stores of Knowledge, I agreed. *Searching for God in America* is a handsome book and somewhat oversized. The dramatic cover stands out, especially when a stack of two hundred copies is placed just inside the doors. A half-dozen book signings promised to be interesting, and I guessed that the book buyers would generally be pleasant. They were. But the exceptions were memorable.

At one store, in Glendale, the store manager warned me upon my arrival that a young woman had already been in to berate the store for involving itself "in God." The cover and the stacked books had caught her eye. PBS came in for some abuse as well. The manager hoped she'd had her say and had moved on.

But she came back. A very angry person, she emerged from the line to demand in an agitated voice what God was I searching for? I have had some experience in deflecting anger. A half-dozen years as a radio talk-show host does have its benefits—and I responded not with an answer but with a question: "Have you seen the show?"

She had not, and that admission seemed to deflate her—for a moment, at least. Within a minute, though, she was furious again. She slammed a book down, repeatedly in fact, as her unfocused but vigorous objections poured out: Religion kills people. Religious leaders are frauds. Authors like me are "God-whores," selling fraud to make money.

It was an incredible burst of venom, directed at me not because of the shows I had made—she hadn't even seen them—or what I'd written in my book—she hadn't read it. But she was ready to launch, and launch she did.

There's not much to do in that situation except remain patient and wait for the storm to abate. It did. With a final slam of the book, she stomped off and did not return.

The signing resumed, and many, many kind people came forward not only to present a book for signing but also to give encouragement. It would have been more productive if they could have encouraged the woman, but not only was she gone, she was probably also too scary to approach. As essayist Joseph Epstein has observed, hot-tempered and crazy people tend to get their way because the effort to engage them is so exhausting. And it can be frightening. Individuals who act irrationally, and especially those willing to raise their voices or use profanity or the wild swings of false accusation—techniques that seem to mark the marginally paranoid—shout or pout their way through life. Good-souled folks, especially those who are gentle, give way.

Not wanting to have a confrontation in a store with a line of customers waiting patiently, I did not want to engage the woman. But I've reflected since then that perhaps I ought to have girded up and stood my ground. It may have been the moment when this obviously troubled and deeply unhappy individual could have witnessed anger met with acceptance and concern. Instead, I simply remained outside of her drama. She left, I suspect, because I'm practiced at the professional distancing of television journalism. She wasn't bothering me, so she left.

Less than an hour later I was on my way to the Santa Monica store, even more apprehensive about "the public" at this stop, given Santa Monica's well-earned reputation for radical politics and confrontation. It's not called "the People's Republic" for no reason, and the arrival of a locally well-known conservative television host promoting a book that is explicitly evangelical was almost certain to draw a couple of oddballs.

Luckily, the first person to arrive was a middle-aged African American woman who was on her church's evangelism committee. She believed that my experience in meeting and conversing with leaders of non-Christian faiths might help equip her for dealing with individuals of those faiths whom she might encounter in her ministry. Soon a semicircle of diverse believers and nonbelievers had formed around the book table discussing God and His pattern in history.

Into this conversation stepped an older man with a kind demeanor. He had a package for me—some tracts by and a videotaped recording of Madalyn Murray O'Hair, a militant atheist who had gained notoriety in the U.S. in the 1960s. Because this gentleman was not obviously angry, I did engage him. Why, I asked, did he care whether or not I believed in God? It was no bother to him. Why did he object to a television series on theology? He didn't have to watch it. And what happened to O'Hair's son, Bill Murray? Hadn't he become quite the Christian witness? And hadn't Ms. O'Hair vanished, suspected by many of skipping town with more than a half-million bucks in organizational dollars?

His answer to all questions, repeated many times over the next hour, was that he hated to see Pat Robertson and others manipulate people, and that religion always manipulated people.

Well, since my friend from the evangelism committee was standing there, I pointed to her and said that she didn't look manipulated or unhappy. And I pointed to a quiet and obviously sweet grandmotherly type and repeated the assertion—she doesn't look manipulated or unhappy. Why, then, try and bother all these apparently happy believers?

Well, my atheist acquaintance did not want to argue that. He wanted to argue that religious belief was delusional. And so he did, with about a half-dozen convinced Christians. He held his ground but not his good humor. Being challenged by so many believers who felt that they were in fact not manipulated automatons quickly ruined his day and caused his temper to hemorrhage. He left muttering, an atheist who could not dent anyone's religious belief that day.

This entire exchange had been of immense interest to everyone involved, except perhaps the store manager who had stockpiled hundreds of books and sold only six. Perhaps an energetic conversation/debate had not been the best way to encourage shoppers to pause at a book table. But it had been a challenge offered, accepted, and met. I was happy. Books can be sold on any day.

The drive home took over an hour, and I reviewed the day's events in some detail. Here is the bottom line: Unhappy, miserable people want to fight. They live for an argument and for the petty triumphs that such verbal battles can bring. It is, perhaps, the only way in which they can feel connected with others. Angry people cannot be in close relationships with God. He will not allow anger to consume people.

Test this out. Identify the *least* angry people you know—those least likely to raise their voices, to confront, to have their blood boil. More than a few names will surface. Ask yourself if you can imagine any of these gentle people stark, raving mad—shouting and screaming and making a scene. If you have picked well, the idea should be somewhat humorous, so incompatible will the idea of anger and these faces be.

Then ask yourself, Do these people believe in God? Specifically, are they Christians?

My guess is that most will be Christians. There will be exceptions.

Many nonbelievers will point to some fairly famous screamers among Christian leadership, and I cannot deny that there are those in the leadership of believers who seem deeply angry and that this attitude is profoundly in opposition to the gospel ethic.

But the vast majority of folks who ask the question and are open to its results will find my guess confirmed by their experience.

Anger and confrontation cannot remain long in the life of a believer. A violent temper does not vanish overnight, of course. I have a volcanic temper that issues forth in massive eruptions on at least an annual basis. But it has gone away bit by bit as I've grown more attentive to God's Word and His call on my life.

Believers trying hard to follow God must abandon anger. It cannot coexist with the commandment to "love one another . . . as I have loved you," or "to love your neighbor as yourself." It can mature into firmness and a considerate compassion, but it cannot remain the wild, unfocused hate or desire to injure or avenge yourself.

The most miserable people I have ever known have been similar only in this respect: They have nurtured and loved their enmity toward others. They had a list, inscribed with the names of those who had done them wrong and deserved retribution. The angry are a vengeful bunch.

I do not believe that it always requires a trained counselor to tackle anger. (I don't believe counselors are inevitable in most situations. Friends and leaders are the key, and the answers are available long before anger becomes pathological.)

Burton is a small town near where I grew up in northern Ohio. It is home to a wonderful event—an annual maple-syrup festival. When the maples are tapped and the sap pours out through the spigots, the town organizes to receive thousands of Buckeyes eager for pancakes and syrup, fresh maple candy, and hard maple sugar figures. A day at the maple sugar festival may not be healthy, but it's awfully good.

It's such a low-tech operation, the collection of sap. The faucet is tapped in, opened, and a bucket is hung underneath. It takes some time for the sap to drain and the bucket to fill. But there's no high-tech wizardry involved. Tap, hammer, bucket— that's it.

Angry people need a tap, a hammer, and a bucket. These tools can come in the form of one person or many. Low-tech, but hard work. Befriending—or tapping—an angry person requires first getting past the discomfort of association with an unpleasant man or woman. And it will require some gentle and some not so gentle knocks at their exteriors—punching through delusion and putting up with some rages. And it will require time to let the anger roll out and be collected. It's not a one-time operation either but a commitment that can extend years and years.

Perhaps a psychologist or a psychiatrist out there will object that I have vastly oversimplified the problem of anger. And perhaps I have. But the ideas that the promotion of basic virtues and the remedy of basic vices have no connection to laypeople is wrongheaded. Our culture has made basic human problems seem overwhelmingly complex at times. It's not hard to spot angry people. I guarantee you the family and acquaintances of the folks in my bookstore encounters know well that she and he are deeply angry people. We all know, in fact, the people in our lives who need ministry too. And that ministry is not that hard to figure out, though it may be hard to do and though we may convince ourselves there are excuses for inaction.

Misery depends on isolation. Connection to others and especially to a community of others threatens misery's fuel supply, which is anger and disappointment in equal parts. Christians are obliged to seek and find those consumed by that anger. The defense of belief is not merely an intellectual exercise. In fact, it is not mostly an intellectual exercise. It is about living a life of faith, and this sort of engagement is part of such a life of service.

Again and again the problem of the Embarrassed Believer rises up, but especially in the context of battling or defusing anger. If folks don't know you are a believer, how can they be expected to connect your personality to the gospel? Let me put it another way. Early in this chapter I asked you to consider those among your acquaintances who were the least likely to lose their tempers. And I suggested that they are likely to be Christians. Here's the problem. If you made a list and there are some question marks on it as to whether your nominee in the category of self-control is a Christian, then embarrassment has scored another win if in fact your friend is a Christian.

No, the faith cannot be spread by the silent. And it cannot be defended by the shy. And defended it must be, because all around us the idea of Christian belief is under assault, both subtle and obvious.

THERE IS A DIFFERENCE BETWEEN MYTH AND TRUTH   13

In the summer of 1996, on the third floor of the Royal British Columbia Museum, there was an exhibit on the "First Peoples" of western Canada. Visitors traveling through the exhibit will encounter many displays devoted to the "cosmology" of the Indians of the region. I was struck by the dilemma facing the exhibit designer and how he or she resolved it.

It is safe to say that the designer did not believe that those "first peoples" had a theology that was and is true. But to state as much with particularity would probably clash with the designer's sense of the expectation of tolerance. So rather than simply describe what the Indians of the Northwest believed, the explanatory wall note stated:

> To understand the world, people create a mythology to explain their universe. A system in which the relationships between people, nature, and the supernatural are presented as symbols is called a cosmology. With dance and song, masks can provide images that bring a cosmology to life.

In that amazing first sentence is a summary of many modern elites' attitudes toward religion: "To understand the world, people create a mythology to explain their universe."

Do you suppose there was a debate on the phrasing of that sentence? It is not at all hesitant: *people create mythology*. As the word "some" is omitted, we must assume the designer's view is that *all* people who have a "cosmology" created it. The implication: There is no God who creates people, only people creating gods: All gods alike. All cosmologies equally false. The designer is certainly P.C. But more than P.C., he or she is quite hostile to Christianity.

In the world of exhibit design, some "cosmologies" are not just false. They are also repellent. Another corridor in the exhibit is designed to

elicit an extraordinarily negative view of Christendom's missions to the
Indians:

> Native culture, with extravagant rituals, including feigned cannibalism,
> struck the Victorian mind as the ultimate in depravity and debauchery.
> It was felt that only European civilization and religion could redeem the
> Indians. Accordingly, a number of missionaries sought to establish them-
> selves; some succeeded beyond expectations, others were ignored or dri-
> ven out.

Here the apparent text cleverly conveys another unspoken subtext:
Christianity is a "European," indeed a "Victorian" religion. Far from
being universal and external in its claims and reach, Christianity is a
small thing, like an empire, subject to growth and retreat as relative
forces ebb and flow. Christianity's origins in the Middle East and Asia
Minor and its early spread in Africa are ignored. The designer is either
ignorant or on a mission against the missionaries.

And just in case the dense visitor missed the point, there was a case
displaying a shattered mask opposite a wall-length picture of a bleak-
looking missionary settlement. The text accompanying the mask read:

> My grandmother told me that when Christianity came, her uncle went
> down to the beach and burned everything. He had heard that the Lord
> will not receive you if you still look to your treasures.
>
> —a Kitamaat woman

Thus the story of the missionaries collapsed into a new fable:
Christianity was the destroyer of all that was old and traditional.

This exhibit underscored how it is now unremarkable to witness the
assault on Christianity among Western elites. There is no parallel for
any other religion. But because Christianity propelled the civilization
and growth of North America, and because the elites of North
America have grown to love things incompatible with Christian belief,
the denigration of Christianity is now commonplace. Indeed, given
what some elites believe and practice, that denigration is compulsory.

My shock at this display may startle nonbelievers. If that's you, please
understand that I believe the claims of Christianity to be true, and not

in some watered-down touchy-feely relativistic sense. I mean *true*. The Gospels record the real events of Jesus of Nazareth, who is the Christ, who was crucified, died, and was buried.

And He rose from the dead and ascended into heaven.

And He will *judge* the living and the dead.

And there are some passages in the gospel that explicitly condition an individual's eternal happiness on the belief in Jesus as the Christ. And to many thoughtful Christians, these passages require the conclusion that absent such a belief in the atoning death of Christ and His resurrection, an individual will suffer horribly and eternally.

Now at least those skeptics with a reasonable degree of intelligence will see how the text of this exhibit offends me. It asserts as true that which I consider to be false. My reaction to it is the same as my reaction to other propaganda—disgust mixed with amusement.

In the days before the Soviet Union collapsed and its archives became available, I would have had the same reaction to individuals arguing moral equivalence between the West and the East. Assertions this stupid are hard to take seriously beyond the level of disgust and amusement, but the stakes were obviously so great in the days of global competition between Soviet tyranny and American freedom that defenders of the truth had to rally themselves to recognize the seriousness of intellectual silliness.

First, an intellectual battle was waged around the danger posed by an expansionist Soviet Union. Then the political will of the country required stealing to carry through on what was a very difficult political program—deployment of new nuclear missiles in Europe and the announcement of a controversial Strategic Defense Initiative. Confronted by this massive show of political and economic resolve, leaders in the Soviet Union attempted a restructuring that would allow their atrophied economy to compete. That restructuring opened the crack that allowed the accumulated desire for freedom on the part of millions to quickly cause the internal collapse of Leninism.

Throughout this glorious and amazing process, there were defenders of the "moral equivalence" school at work in the West. They are still around, though their "causes" have shifted. Their propaganda was eventually revealed as just plain stupid. But the damage it accomplished was real.

So, too, is the damage accomplished by the dominant culture's "equivalence" theory in matters such as these museum notes. I do not object at all to the debate about God's existence, and I certainly do not want to give any aid or comfort to individuals seeking to "establish" an official creed or church in the U.S. or anywhere. But the de facto and in fact cowardly elevation of disbelief to that very status of "established church" is profoundly wrong, as wrong as was the decades-long indecision by some on where evil resided in the world's governments.

Believers must be willing to engage at the level of "museum notes." Frequently the backhanded slap at faith will appear in a newspaper or a broadcast. For years Christians have shrugged off these slights as inevitable. Some have even counseled "turn the other cheek." But that instruction—and it is a command with a context—is not an invitation to allow the culture of disbelief to destroy God's people. Challenges offered, from the small assumptions of the museum walls to the loud and abusive scorn that the elite media heap upon believers, must be met. It's an uncomfortable prospect but not a particularly difficult one.

The very act of engagement profits the faith. Here's one example. In the spring of 1997, the Promise Keepers returned to Los Angeles. On two successive days, more than forty-five thousand men attended a Promise Keepers rally at the Los Angeles Coliseum. Many of these men came from Orange County, less than an hour's drive for many of them. The two newspapers that serve the entire Orange County area—the *Orange County Register* and the *Los Angeles Times*—did not carry a combined six inches on the two-day event.

More than a few Christians complained, and the *Register's* "ombudsman" responded in print. "Does the *Register* ignore mainstream Christians and their activities while giving excessive coverage to peripheral religious issues?" asked the ombudsman. "Some readers think so," he concluded.

But how did the paper's religion editor respond? "Events outside Orange County are always a difficult issue for us, no matter what the subject," said Michael Hewitt (no relation, thank goodness). "Paperwide, our coverage of events outside the county is generally restricted to sports. For instance we also didn't cover the Cinco de Mayo festival at the L.A. Coliseum Sunday, which no doubt drew thousands from Orange County as well."

Do you see what the answer is? The Promise Keepers and a Cinco de Mayo festival *are the same thing* in the eyes of the *religion* editor of one of California's preeminent newspapers. A party-festival carnival is the same thing as a giant worship service! It's an absurd equivalency. People are murdered around the globe for their faith. The First Amendment to the U.S. Constitution testifies that the right to "free exercise" of religious belief is paramount in our country's origins, but an editor tosses off a comparison of worship to a party.

The key is not that the paper has a serious flaw in its understanding of religion. Rather, it is that the demand of an accounting by believers forced that flow into the light of day. An attitude was exposed, like the attitude in the museum wall notes.

Unless believers have the courage to undertake this demand for accountability and fairness, it will not occur. And while it may be an uncomfortable job, it's not a dangerous one, at least in the sense of real danger and real courage.

ACTUALLY, IT'S NOT THAT HARD

We have MacArthur Fellowships to recognize genius. And there is a Templeton Prize to honor folks who have advanced religion in the world. Nobel Prizes are bestowed on the globe's greatest in matters of medicine, physics, and chemistry, literature, economics, and peace. The Pulitzer honors newspaper work; the Oscar crowns the movie business; the Emmy marks achievement in television; the Tony, achievement in theater; the Grammy in music. The Wilbur Awards honor the defense of religion in the American media.

There are gold, silver, and bronze medals in the Olympics, Stanley Cups and green jackets and other sorts of plaques and markers in sports. Gold watches mark long service. Honorary degrees mark commencements. Monuments mark dead achievers.

Men and women like to recognize achievement. We want to have a means to separate significant achievement from the routine.

Even among honors and awards there is a hierarchy. Countries establish an internal hierarchy of honor. Among the toppers: the Order of Leopold (Belgium), the Supreme Order of the Chrysanthemum (Japan), the Legion of Honor (France), the Order of Pius (The Vatican), and the Victoria Cross (Great Britain).

To an American, there is clearly a highest military honor: the Medal of Honor. It was authorized by Congress in 1861 as the first permanent military decoration. The Medal of Honor goes to heroes who exhibit gallantry in action.

It is widely and correctly viewed as the highest military honor in the United States because its predicate is physical courage in defense of others.

Certainly there are many courageous people who battle illness or tough circumstances. Certainly there are still American soldiers, sailors, and pilots who are displaying courage even as I write this. Certainly thousands of police and firefighters will, on the day you read this, engage in courageous conduct.

But "courage" is still a devalued word because we attach it to so many things that are, obviously, not courageous.

Politicians routinely talk of "courageous stands" when all that is at risk is a few votes and possibly an elected office and a stable salary. The worst that can happen to a "courageous" politician is sudden retirement.

And writers (and reviewers) are fond of the word "courageous." It's often applied to writing that might otherwise be thought simply vulgar or even pornographic.

Similarly, artists with "edgy" art claim that the risk of harsh reviews or small audiences entitles them to the title of courageous.

For clarity's sake, let's go to an unlikely source. Peter Hopkirk is a journalist and an author. Two of his books provided me with many hours of entertainment: *The Great Game* and *Like Hidden Fire.* The former charts a century of English attempts to control Central Asia. The latter reviews the struggle for mastery of the same geography between imperial Germany and imperial England during World War I. Each book is a narrative of scores of individual adventures across the violent and desolate reaches of vast desert regions.

An example: Capt. Oskar von Niedermayer chose July 1915 to travel by foot and horse from Isfahan in Persia to Kabul, Afghanistan. He and his party trekked across a brutal desert in summer because he needed to make an effort to bring the Kabul government into the Great War on the Kaiser's side. Hopkirk recounts:

> Travelling by night to escape what Niedermayer called "the terrible fire of the Persian sun," as well as the attention of British spies, they frequently lost their way in the darkness. This brought unexpected hazards. On their third night out of Isfahan they made a chilly discovery when they found themselves riding through "hundreds of poisonous snakes which had come out to hunt." After one horse had collapsed and died from a snake bite, Niedermayer related, "we had to send ahead men clad in leather leggings and armed with whips to clear the way." The following morning, apart from their tracks in the sand, there was no sign of snakes; instead the camp was crawling with giant scorpions which crept

into the men's clothing to escape the heat. "Every piece of clothing," Niedermayer wrote, "had to be shaken carefully before we got dressed."[1]

Seven weeks after starting out, they arrived in Kabul from the desert—"walking skeletons," wrote Niedermayer. "The courage, skill and tenacity displayed by Niedermayer and his companions are worthy of our highest admiration," concluded the official British war historian.

Niedermayer earned the respect and admiration of his mortal opponents because of a remarkable feat of tenacity combined with bravery. His own life was at stake. The dangers real. The gamble was large, and the prize was equal to the wager.

Really, compared to such an adventure, what are the "courageous" acts of today? Don't speeches by Oscar recipients seem a little silly?

I recount just one episode of indisputably courageous behavior to suggest that believers really have grown pretty timid. Many American Christians have often abandoned bold behavior because of a concern with worldly opinion. The honors and decorations and mementos of success that crown modern careers are generally unavailable to people who boldly talk about faith. Athletes are the last significant exception, but medals based on physical performance are not forfeited because of expressions of faith. I suspect, though, that the first Oscar recipient to witness to his or her religious belief after receiving the statue could assume that no return trip would ever occur. Even in the ordinary world of day-to-day business, promotion and proselytism are not allies.

Still, so what? Most Christians are familiar with a passage from Paul's letter to the Philippians: "But whatever gain I had, I counted as loss for the sake of Christ. Indeed I count everything as loss because of the surpassing worth of knowing Christ Jesus my Lord. For his sake I have suffered the loss of all things, and count them as refuse, in order that I may gain Christ" (Philippians 3:7–8).

A powerful verse, that one. Everything except Christ is rubbish, trash, throwaway stuff.

If this verse seized the minds and hearts of even a handful of

---

1. Peter Hopkirk, *Like Hidden Fire: The Plot to Bring Down the British Empire* (New York: Kodansha, 1997), 123.

Christians, the engines of evangelism would go to warp speed immediately. Consider why: Persons caught by the truth of this verse would know that position and honor have no value, much less any relative value to "the surpassing greatness of knowing Christ Jesus my Lord." Moreover, knowing this, they would want others to know it, too, and they would seize every appropriate opportunity to witness.

Some readers—ardent evangelicals—will see that word— *appropriate*—and fairly shout out "weasel word!" It's a word that, if abused, can expand to cover 99.9 percent of life. I call such words "accordion" words—they expand and contract to meet the needs of the user.

And the word *appropriate* as used in the phrase "appropriate opportunity to evangelize" is an accordion word. Here's what I mean.

Every single waking moment in a believer's life is an opportunity to evangelize if there is a nonbeliever within communicating distance. And since very few people are beyond the reach of a letter, pretty much every moment is an opportunity to evangelize.

"Appropriate" opportunities are a subset of opportunities. Here the debate is endless.

When I spoke on the theme of boldness in witness to a gathering of Christian bookstore owner/operators, the age-old question came from the floor: "Isn't there a danger of turning off people? I just try and let Christ shine through my life." A few minutes later, another owner/ operator stood to urge a much more vigorous proclamation of belief.

I have considered that exchange for a long time. First, the audience was unusual. I assume that all or nearly all Christian bookstore operators are themselves evangelical. It's sort of in the nature of the business. And I seriously doubt that a Christian bookstore owner is ever rightfully labeled an embarrassed believer. So it's not an easy question but rather one that was offered by an individual who felt he had the authority to urge caution.

And the circumstances under which witness can occur are so varied that the prospect of fashioning a general rule is pretty daunting. But there must be some way to voice such a rule.

I came up with this: When the reward of the witness is at least as great as the risk to the church, then witness ought to occur; then witness is appropriate.

Paul himself was aware that while God could not be threatened or in any way damaged, His church could be. "An elder must be blameless," concluded Paul to Titus (Titus 1:6 NIV)—good advice, especially in an age where media think hypocrisy is news and understand hypocrisy to apply principally to people of faith who are not yet fully free of sin (meaning everyone). And it is obvious that the church can be and has been seriously hurt in its efforts to spread the good news of the gospel by charges of hypocrisy. Similarly, "witness" can have a baleful effect if delivered at the wrong time, from the wrong mouth, or with the wrong words.

Assume for a moment that Dan Rather is Christian. (He may or may not be; I don't know.) At one point in his career, Rather signed off a broadcast with the word "courage." Silly at the time, that routine earned Rather no small amount of grief. Had he kept up signing off his broadcast with silly and unintelligible exhortations, he probably wouldn't have held on to his job.

So assume he was a Christian and began concluding his broadcast with: "And may the peace that surpasses all understanding that comes from faith in the resurrected Christ touch and fill you. Good night." I imagine he'd get to do it once or twice, and then would be exited stage left.

Perhaps not. If enough believers (plus nonbelievers attached to the idea of free expression) rallied to his defense, the network might allow Rather to continue in his job; but the TV executives certainly would attempt to sever his tag line.

If Rather asked a pastor, "Should I do this in order to evangelize?" I suspect the answer would be no. Good counsel would encourage Rather to use his position to do good and to choose opportunities to spread the gospel in ways that did not oblige his employers to examine the question of his employment.

An easier example: Say the fellow who types in the scores constantly running during CNN's *Headline News* decided to start "witnessing" by including a Bible verse or two between scores. "Indians 8, Yankees 0—'All have sinned and fall short of the glory of God and are justified freely by his grace through the redemption that came by Jesus Christ' (Romans 3:23–24 NIV). Rangers 6, White Sox 2." That electronic score-board operator would not only lose his job, he would bring derision on the church and would enhance the notion, abundantly popular among elites, that believers are just a group of fanatics, some better camouflaged than others.

Having recognized that there is always a question of when is the "appropriate opportunity" to witness, still the vast number of believers are never in danger of even approaching the border between appropriate and inappropriate. And this is why I began this chapter with a few words about courage.

In the U.S. at the end of the twentieth century it simply does not require courage to witness to one's belief in Christ. It most certainly does require boldness and the defeat of personal timidity. And there is definitely the risk of embarrassment and even financial loss. But there is zero prospect of physical danger from witnessing because of the witness.

(Yes, I know. The act of witnessing in a tough neighborhood can be courageous. But it is not because of the witnessing; it's because of the neighborhood. Delivering groceries is also courageous in such places.)

Discussing one's faith in the wrong country can be physically hazardous. The week before I penned the first draft of this chapter, a missionary was released after two years of captivity in the jungles of South America. It seems missionaries have always been easy targets for local extremists and insecure governments. And as I edit this book, more and more reports are arriving from the Middle East of the worst sorts of massacres of Christians.

After years of hard and often ignored work, Nina Shea's Pueblo Institute and other similarly oriented organizations have captured the occasional attention of the American media in their effort to spark media coverage of religious persecution around the globe. The violence against people of faith because of their faith comes as a shock to many in the American opinion elite because they cannot comprehend anyone taking religion seriously enough either to persecute it or suffer greatly for it. But no matter the depth of American indifference or skepticism, religious persecution of the worst sort is real around the globe, and Christians are often the target.

Not in this country, however, at least not physical persecution. It is doubtful that anyone reading this book in the U.S. will ever have to worry about his or her life or limb if talk turns to faith.

So why the great silence about belief? And why the shocked reaction on the part of so many in the media to *Searching for God in America?* Many of the television reporters who interviewed me in advance of the series' premier could not conceal their surprise that PBS would sponsor such a show. The shock in their voices was telling.

I wrote in the introduction to *Searching for God in America* that the dominant media culture in the United States has silenced God's people by being silent about God. No negative coverage, no war on religion— simply a tyrannical uniformity of indifference. So unbroken has the silence been that it was big news that ABC hired a journalist to be assigned to the religion beat a few years back. *Searching for God in America* was also news, not because of a particular sequence of questions and answers, but because the content generally dealt with God. It was a novel thing. It was news.

It would be news in the workplaces of America if men and women of faith boldly declared as much. It would be news in the bureaucracies of America if believing government workers expressed their faith openly. It would be news if Christian teachers in the public schools of the country concluded that it was time to participate in the campus Bible club without regard to the administration's belief. It would be news if letter writers began to demand from their newspapers an unbiased coverage of the church.

The predicate to all that news, however, is boldness on the part of believers. Not courage, mind you. I hope I have persuaded you of the difference. Boldness is required of the many, not the few.

In this belief I am opposed by one of the writers with whom I dislike finding myself in opposition. Michel de Montaigne's *Essays* were written more than four hundred years ago, but they remain one of the greatest works of literature to have survived the grinding of time. The fifty-sixth essay concerns prayer. Here is a sample of his opinion.

We must not mix God into our actions except with reverence and with devout and respectful attention. His word is too divine to have no other use than to exercise our lungs and please our ears; it should be uttered from the conscience and not from the tongue. It is not right that a shop apprentice, amid his vain and frivolous thoughts, should entertain himself and play with it.

Nor assuredly is it right to see the holy book of the sacred mysteries of our belief bandied about a hall or a kitchen. Formerly they were myster-ies; at present they are sports and pastimes.

Montaigne lived and worked even as the Reformation swept Europe and upset all ordered things. And in such times it is easier to under-stand a reluctance to allow matters of theological conviction to be debated "in kitchens and halls." Such debates could lead to swordplay.

And while I am most definitely the "shop apprentice" Montaigne refers to, I know these conditions have long since passed. We have the swordplay and gunplay without any theological disputes whatsoever. The culture is silent about God; but it is raucously noisy on sin, and the sound is usually applause.

A beginning has been made. Bill Bennett opened the door. Stephen Carter was next; he is a Yale Law professor whose book, *The Culture of Disbelief,* walked through that opening. Others have followed. *First Things*—a magazine—and Michael Medved, a movie critic, have boldly asserted principles associated with and dependent upon deep religious belief. Others are joining up.

The "new paradigm" churches such as Calvary Chapel, Hope Chapel, and the Vineyards are demanding attention by virtue of their impact. Prof. Donald E. Miller of the University of Southern California has published a bracing new book, *Reinventing American Protestantism,* that places these new churches at the center of an evangelical earth-quake for which their pastors make no apologies and for which none are needed.

Boldness certainly has its generals and its allies. Now it needs troops. And as we'll cover later, the generals must really lead, and do so from the heart. But even the greatest leadership cannot rally an empty field. There must be troops. You must be among them.

Declare your faith. Defend it. Dissent from the culture around you when that culture cannot be reconciled with your beliefs. It's really not that hard. No desert crossings. No burning at the stake. Probably not even that much embarrassment.

Fame is the highest ambition of the noblest minds." So said Alexander Hamilton. My conversations over the past couple of years discredit his assertion.

I have enjoyed the fun of politics for most of my forty-two years. Meeting and working with world-historical figures is bracing. As a twenty-two-year old, I spent a few hours a week with Richard Nixon and experienced the enormous charisma that powerful leaders possess—even exiled, disgraced, and formerly powerful leaders as RN was at the time. The Western White House where I worked is gone now, torn down by bureaucrats following someone's idiot directive. But when I had an office there, it overlooked a parking lot through which RN would walk each evening on the way back to his home, Casa Pacifica. Most early evenings I would watch him briskly walk the beginning of the quarter-mile course and would always conclude, "What a life."

I doubt a half-dozen people in this century have led lives as significant as Richard Nixon's. Churchill, Stalin, Eisenhower, Mao, and Nixon each held his country's highest office during both war and peace. All of them were stewards of nuclear arsenals. All shaped history. Perhaps Reagan and Gorbachev are in the same rank; but without leadership in war, the quality of the "fame" is lessened. But the fame of these individuals is such that human culture will and must account for their having lived. Love them or hate them, they cannot be ignored.

Pretty much everything else can be ignored even in the short run. And not only can it be, shortly it will be. The shelf life of even former presidents is pretty short. When I sat down to interview Jimmy Carter a few years ago, it was because he'd written a memoir of his early political life in the South. It was something of a sad occasion for me—just another author selling books. I had the same reaction when Gerald

Ford and I shared a billing at the "High Desert Economic Expo" a few years ago. No doubt my speaking fee was considerably less than his, but what was a former president of the United States doing there?

Enduring fame is, of course, a myth. It doesn't exist. Recall the paragraphs devoted to "chasing after wind" that were quoted earlier in this book. Turn again to Ecclesiastes in the Appendix. Ask yourself, how many know much about Priam and Ajax, Pompey and Augustus, Charlemagne and Leo, Elizabeth or Philip? Of those who do know, how many care? That is, whose lives are touched and changed by knowledge of lives of these epochal historical figures?

I made this argument a few chapters ago, but I repeat it now because we have trouble reminding ourselves of our own insignificance. We are programmed to overrate our importance. So I return to one of the key recognitions we can make in our lives, and it is a recognition critical to the empowerment of the Embarrassed Believer.

Fame always fades. Most of it in relatively short order. All of it eventually. The "big" names of this century that I mentioned earlier will diminish as well. Maybe they'll get a hundred years. Maybe a thousand. But ten thousand years? Of course not. Either the world will have ended in Christ's second coming and no one individual will matter more than anyone else, or it will not have ended yet and no one living now will matter.

Men and women have a tough time accepting their insignificance vis-a-vis each other and human history, however, and spend an enormous amount of time trying to trick themselves into believing it's somehow different for them.

But ask yourself:

Will Madonna matter in fifty years?

When Tom Brokaw eventually dies, how long will you pause to mourn his passing? How long did you pause to mark the passing of John Chancellor, who once held the same job as Brokaw?

Does anyone really believe that Bill Clinton will matter two days after his term ends in 2001?

While writing this book, I happened to share a plane ride to Sacramento with a friend who was on the way to California's capital in order to investigate a run for statewide office. Even two years earlier I would have fallen into an interesting conversation about the mechanics of such a contest—fund-raising, campaign staff, pollsters, media strategy. Instead I keep returning to the question: "Why are you doing this?"

Most politicians cannot answer this forthrightly because it is an embarrassing answer: To "be" someone. To have significance. To matter. To be a "player," part of the mix, part of the game. To achieve applause and respect.

To be famous.

A few have different answers. Driven by a cause, they are seeking office in order to gain power and then attack a problem or an issue.

It was like that during the Cold War. The anticommunists recognized evil. They wanted power in order to defeat evil. Paul Nitze and other cold-warriors were not driven by fame but by purpose.

At the end of this century, political candidates are pretty pale imitations of previous power seekers. The fame they seek is diluted. I asked my friend on the plane, "Who would you rather be in 1996, George Bush or George Will?" The answer was Will, and most political people would answer the same way. Will is more influential at present and will continue to be more influential than Bush. Bush is more significant historically, true enough; but Will has more attention paid to what he says and writes. Bush's real but brief power is not so attractive as Will's very illusory but longer-lasting fame and influence. And both will have equal importance, which is to say none, in a single generation.

"If it's not on television, it hardly matters," is one of Ed Rollins's "rules." Rollins is a fairly repugnant creation of modern media politics— the hired gun who always ends up shooting the folks who hired him. Repellent though he is, this "rule" of his is demonstrably true, at least in the world of modern fameology. Not on TV? Doesn't matter. Period.

Look, I told my friend, what you are thinking of doing makes no sense. It will not bring you fame; politics cannot deliver that anymore. It will not bring you power; only the Governor, the Attorney General, the Speaker of the California Assembly and the President Pro Tem of the California Senate have genuine power in the Golden State. Even if you win, I went on, you are not likely to end up in any of those jobs. So why do it?

"What would you have me do?" he came back. An honest and fair question.

Ambitious people cannot stop being ambitious. And folks who want fame cannot stop wanting it. But it is possible to want fame and to be ambitious in productive ways.

"Run for State Superintendent of School Instruction," I suggested. "You'll have the ability to really change schools. Free the kids from the disasters that are out there in public education." And the conversation followed that course for a while.

I was tempted to say, Make money (which this individual already did and could easily continue to do) and give it away to the poor. But that would not have addressed the desire for fame.

There are only two ways to deal with the desire for fame. Destroy it or control it to good ends. With my friend I chose the latter. I followed James Madison's logic when he wrote the tenth essay in the series known as the *Federalist Papers*. Factions—parties—were dangerous, wrote Madison. Either we destroy them, or we control them. As destroying them would involve either destroying liberty or converting all people to one-of-a-kind opinions, Madison gave up trying to destroy factions and set about devising a government to control the inevitable development of political parties. With my friend's ambition in mind, I set out on the same path—control the ambition.

I ought to have encouraged her to try to destroy it. Given its illusory quality, given that fame cannot last and hardly matters when it exists, I should have counseled, "Forget this nonsense."

That is what Thomas à Kempis counseled. In the *Imitation of Christ*, he urged people to flee from the courts of kings. Why? I can only guess. I suspect because of the diversions, the vanities, the sinfulness, and the unhappiness that generally surrounds power. I worked inside the White House only briefly but long enough to know this is true in America today. (Where is former White House Chief of Staff Don Regan right now? And the "three blind mice"—his deputies—who were for a time in the 1980s so powerful?) And history teaches us it has always been so.

I interview powerful people nearly every week. Very few strike me as happy in the way that I think of the genuine thing: joyful and peaceful, at rest and content. The famous are awfully busy and usually cranky. Not the attributes of happiness.

Not so for the guests on *Searching for God in America*. Chuck

Colson, Roberta Hestenes, Thomas Keating, the Dalai Lama, Seyyed Hossein Nasr, Neal Maxwell, Harold Kushner, and Cecil Murray comprise a very disparate group of people. I hold them up as eight completely different folks, in fact united only in that they are passionate about God. And with one exception, they struck me as happy and content. Not one was on the way to somewhere else, though obviously some of them had career changes ahead. (Roberta Hestenes was president of Eastern College at the time of the interview; she is now pastor of Solano Beach Presbyterian Church in San Diego County, California.)

I contrast this group of God-seeking people with any group of eight fame-centered or power-centered folks you'd care to nominate. In which group do you suppose the joy is the greatest?

I have interviewed many of the rich and famous. In fact, one of my favorite guest categories is the Hollywood "activist." I've had great fun questioning and arguing with the likes of Oliver Stone and Rob Reiner.

But I remain amazed by a glimpse accorded to me of the inner life of the hugely successful celebrity by Richard Dreyfuss in early 1997.

Near the end of a two-hour interview, I asked Dreyfuss if he was satisfied with his considerable accomplishments. Though his politics are unpersuasive, I've never not loved a Dreyfuss movie that I'd seen. He's Curt Henderson and Mr. Holland, for goodness' sake. Mr. Blockbuster in *Jaws* and *Close Encounters*. An Oscar winner for *The Goodbye Girl*.

So I was surprised when he very emphatically and repeatedly stressed that he'd give it all back if he could have a normal life as a history teacher. It turns out he'd like his privacy back. A newspaper account of this exchange later mocked the very idea that a celebrity genuinely disliked his fame, but I am certain Dreyfuss was speaking sincerely.

My conclusion? Richard Dreyfuss is a talented man of great intellect and good intentions. He's successfully battled addiction and won, and his career continues to allow him excellent roles. But he's not happy. He's got money, fame, and even power. But he's not happy.

God-centered people are happy. Genuine Christians are happy.

Not that God-centered people reject fame and power. They do not. Fame and power are means, though, not ends. Those who lose sight of that crucial distinction have abandoned their focus.

How to know whether people of faith are genuinely God-centered?

I think a good test is to apply the same question to them as I directed to my friend on the Sacramento-bound plane: Why do what you are about to do? People of faith will answer quickly, and that answer will in one way or another reference God: "It's God's call on my life," or "I'm bringing God's word to people," or "I'm ministering according to the gospel." Sure, some will be able to cloak their own ambition in an insincere description of mission. But that's a hard trick to pull off for very long.

The highest ambition of the noble minds I have encountered over the past two years was service: Service to God's will that displayed itself in service to fellow humans. It was Chuck Colson in truly awful prisons and Roberta Hestenes in famine-relief camps. It was Thomas Keating teaching a quiet audience the ways of contemplative prayer and Seyyed Hossein Nasr reminding the West of the need for the sacred, the Dalai Lama serving the cause of the Tibetan people, and Harold Kushner bringing comfort through books and speeches to folks as badly bruised as he had been by tragedy. It was Neal Maxwell literally giving his retirement in the service of the Mormon Church, and Cecil Murray walking away from a burning plane into seminary so that one day he could walk through burning streets proclaiming a gospel of peace.

All of them have some measure of fame, and all of them have some measure of power; but all of them count those things as either accidents or tools. I do not believe the non-Christians among them have chosen correctly as to how God has worked and is working in the universe. But all have correctly chosen to serve others rather than themselves.

And each carries an air of purpose and confidence that is not often found. Those attributes ought to call out to folks fervent in their belief but afraid to express it. Expression of faith through service may be the easiest means to the end of witness. The confusion often occurs that witness must be verbal. Usually it is. But silent service can be as bold as the loudest speech. And I am convinced that the most genuine believers cannot be found separated from a life of service.

16

"You Cannot Reach the Formless Except through Form": A Very Brady Sequel Meets the Talmud and the Koran

N ow we must return to the business of preparation—the hard work of shedding embarrassment in exchange for confidence.

My conversations with religious leaders equipped me with stories and theological insights, history, and a few great phrases. This last category is interesting because as I explained in my earlier chapter on Velcro, the phrases that stayed with me even two years after completing an interview must have carried with them a particular force, because they lasted. They stuck.

One phrase resonated from my interview with Dr. Seyyed Hossein Nasr, the distinguished Islamic scholar: "You cannot reach the formless except through form." In the course of dozens of interviews and appearances promoting the series and the book, I would almost always be asked, "What did you learn?" Many things, obviously, some of which have already surfaced in this book. But I always responded to this repeated question and—after reserving for myself the right to expand the answer—I routinely would cite Dr. Nasr's imperative: "You cannot reach the formless except through form." I thought his warning was particularly relevant to Christians who are in danger of getting lost in New Age emptiness and emotionalism.

I think this thought struck me as memorable, and in fact stayed with me, because it summarized, and eloquently, a notion that I'd been struggling to articulate but hadn't been able to convey in succinct fashion. In the first book I wrote, a decade before *Searching for God in America,* I quoted from English author E. M. Forster: "I suggest that the only books that influence us are those for which we are reading, and which have gone a little further down our own particular path than we have got ourselves. You are being influenced when you say 'I might have written that myself if I hadn't been so busy.'" When Dr. Nasr expressed his rule, I was influenced. I agree with his conclusion, and I believe that his statement is a rebuke to so much that passes for spirituality in our day.

In an interview I conducted for my Los Angeles program, Rabbi Adin Steinsaltz, perhaps the greatest Talmud scholar in a few hundred years, asserted that the problem with spirituality in the United States was that Americans wanted "a good five-cent religion." On the cheap, he was saying. Immediately. Overnight. Fast-food mysticism to go with our fast-food culture.

Rabbi Steinsaltz seemed to me to state an obvious truth, and Dr. Nasr explained the reason why the people described in that truth— Americans—would ultimately be frustrated in their desire. No small irony there: An Israeli rabbi and an Iranian-expatriate Islamic scholar provided the intellectual bookends, or prompts, for a diagnosis crucial to American believers and seekers alike, especially Christians.

Here's the problem: Americans in record numbers are interested in "mysticism." Big word, *mysticism*. It's one of those accordion words I discussed earlier. It can mean hundreds of different things.

Unfortunately, to many it means a set of sensations—actual physical experiences. Mystical experiences seem almost always to include sensory experiences. People "feel things," hear things, see things. Or they want to. The desire is to go "other-worldly," to be transported. Didn't Aquinas levitate? Can't the Dalai Lama read minds? What about all those near-death, out-of-body experiences?

Can we do that too? That sounds neat.

Here's a sobering thought: Of the thousands who got to hear Jesus preach in New Testament days, only twelve were called to the closeness signified by the title "apostle."

Of those twelve apostles, only three were privileged to witness the Transfiguration. Those unfamiliar with the Transfiguration can find a record of it in Luke 9:28–36.

Jesus was not in the business of passing out mystical experiences. In fact, His closest followers appeared to have spent a great deal of time in rather ordinary, pedestrian pastimes such as walking, teaching, and fishing. There's just not much in Scripture about personal and inward mystical experiences.

Saint Paul had such an experience, absolutely. He told of being transported to "The Third Level of Heaven." And the entire Book of Revelation is exactly that—a mystical vision given to John.

But consider the numbers. The odds are very much against you or me having such an experience, such a revelation.

Pentecostals reading along with me are beginning to grow uneasy about now. They can relax. The gifts of the Spirit are very different, indeed, from what the modern mysticism seeker is seeking. Visions and voices—those are "the gold in them thar hills" to the mysticism seekers.

There certainly is gold in them thar hills. But if you are going to get it, it's going to take a lot of work and, I suspect, a lot of time.

"You cannot reach the formless without the form."

A married couple who were missionaries once appeared before our church's congregation to give a report on their efforts. For year upon year they had worked among the poorest of the poor in a faraway place. Then they had miraculously been allowed to continue their mission work in a country very hostile to Christian workers—so hostile, in fact, that I cannot even now write about it with more specificity.

Smack in the middle of their testimony came this bombshell: They had sold their home and left their lives behind because the woman had had "a vision." She'd been in prayer, and the Lord had shown her their ultimate destination, as clear as a bell.

This sort of testimony doesn't go over well with me. I'm a lawyer who likes evidence, a Presbyterian who likes the *Book of Order;* but I had to believe that she had seen this vision. She and her husband acted on the vision at great risk and enormous discomfort. (They bought one-way air tickets and had no return money. Missionaries do these sorts of things.)

So who am I to sit there in the air-conditioned comfort of my very orderly church and say visions and voices don't exist? So I don't.

But I do say that visions are most likely to be authentic when accompanied by personal sacrifice preceded by years of basic training.

When Rabbi Steinsaltz stated that Americans wanted a good five-cent religion, I think he was alluding to the desire for visions and voices right away—the wish for a kind of cosmic entertainment, a ticket to Six Flags over Heaven.

What Dr. Nasr was saying—and he was addressing the Mysticism Now crowd—was "forget it." No visions and voices for the lazy, the inexperienced, the insincere. And by the way, probably none at all for the young.

Here's the complete exchange with Dr. Nasr:

HUGH HEWITT: In some of your writings you point out false spiritualism in the United States. Is that a result of just putting on one religion after another?

SEYYED HOSSEIN NASR: It's the result of several things. It's, first of all, the result of trying to eat a walnut without the shell—that is, trying to reject the formal in the name of the formless and without first possessing the form. What has attracted Americans, especially to Zen Buddhism, is the iconoclasm . . . burning the Buddhist scrolls and tearing down the Buddha image and so forth. This appeals to a lot of people from a Christian or Jewish setting who are coming out of an unhappy religious experience in childhood or something like that. And they say, "Oh, finally I can throw all of these things away and just concentrate on illumination," which is totally absurd. Absolutely absurd. Because you cannot reach the formless except through form. The main reason for this wishy-washy spiritualism, which doesn't get anywhere except to make some people rich, is that rejection of the forms which God has revealed Himself.

HUGH HEWITT: You cannot reach the formless without the form. Will you expand on that a little bit?

SEYYED HOSSEIN NASR: Yes. You have, for example, these great sages of Islam and Hinduism who have oftentimes spoken much more openly about the formless, about the one that transcends all forms. And you can hear them speaking: "My heart is open to every religion. It's the temple, and a mosque, and a synagogue. And let the gazelle roam in it." And, "Mine is the religion of love." They've all spoken about this—the Persian and Arab mystics, and Sufis, and in India, Hindu seers like Rama Krishna. But how did they get there, to be able to say such a thing? They lived for years and years as devout Hindus or Muslims, and they never ceased to be devout Hindus or Muslims until they died. We forget that. We forget that someone like Rumi never missed a prayer for every year of his life since he was a teenager until he died. Or in Arabic, the same way. And we want to repeat the utterances which they make after having traversed the whole path and reached the top of the mountain, without having done the mountain climbing.

In Christianity, sacred form is the rite that is given by Christ. It's the Eucharist. Eucharist was taken by all traditional Christians over the centuries. But in the thirteenth century, the great German mystic Meister Eckart said, "I swam in the ocean of divinity until I went beyond the Trinity." And he was castigated by the church for having said that. He said he swam in the ocean of divine Godhead. Now, he went to mass every day. So the form was always there. It was the inner reality which the form led to, which is beyond form itself.

The great mystery of religious forms is that they're not closed forms, like man-made forms. They open inwardly to the infinite. But the religious forms are extremely important, because they're the only doors that we have to the infinite. So once we reject them and try to go for the walnut without the shell, we can never have access to it. And we usually have to satisfy ourselves with the psychologization of the spiritual.

Get the picture? Christians in the United States are especially vulnerable to the false promise of mystical experience since their traditional churches have been involved in a collapse of confidence.

So where did this desire for mystical experience come from anyway? Some are obviously seeking communion with God, the experience of His real presence, the force of His love. These things are fairly easy to obtain, I think, with an initial submission of the will and with an earnest request. Among Christians, there is a famous "sinners' prayer" that is sincerely urged on nonbelievers at evangelical events: "Lord, I'm a sinner. I know I am. I need you. Please, Jesus, come into my life. Forgive my sins. Save me." There are other versions.

Millions and millions of people have prayed that prayer and experienced incredible feelings immediately thereafter. Conversion-experience accounts provide thrilling, captivating reading.

Millions and millions more have been further along in a life of sincere seeking and can and do experience the real presence of God in prayer and daily life. I am among them. I know, with rock-solid certainty, when I have drawn close to God. It is impossible not to know it.

But I do not yearn for visions or voices. Not only would they distract and divert, they could be very upsetting. What if God showed a visionary hell? In fact, I'm pretty happy not glimpsing the full glory of God. The biblical precedents for such experiences uniformly involve falling down and trembling.

Would you go to a zoo on the day the bars fell down and the tiger was free to wander about? There are real, rational limits to an ordinary person's capacity to experience God.

With training, that capacity can increase.

Plenty of obvious examples abound. I used to run long distances at respectable speeds. But it took months of training to achieve the ability to run a marathon. On the first day of training, I'd run a half-mile and walk a half-mile. Five months later, I ran a marathon. In between—hundreds of miles.

So it is with God. He can and will give the asker the answer, and complete salvation is only a moment away. But glimpsing His immensity is different from claiming His salvation. The latter requires a second. A lifetime's practice only begins the former.

The reason this is not obvious in the West is twofold.

Older Americans grew up in a culture that did not allow them the leisure to go looking for mountaintop experiences. The very idea of "vision quests" on Main Street would have been unthinkable in the middle of the Depression and World War II. Sure, as my conversations with Trappist monk Thomas Keating showed, such quests did occur then, but in very small numbers. So for part of our population, the difficulty of mystical experience is obscured because not many people have thought about it much or have pursued it.

For boomers and those younger, it is exactly the opposite problem. The culture of the sixties birthed the widespread use of drugs. Even those who did not use drugs at all or only sparingly or only the lesser forms know the lingo of narcotic experience. Even descriptions now bathed in irony, such as "tripping," conveyed distinct ideas of surreal, "otherly" experiences.

A fairly funny movie—*A Very Brady Sequel*—had its theater and video runs while I was writing this book. As a total low-brow when it comes to movies—I will see anything that isn't rated NR or isn't a horror/slasher film—I went to *A Very Brady Sequel*. I laughed and laughed as the film was a parody of the decade of the seventies, which had consumed my generation and its dignity long ago.

I particularly enjoyed a sequence where a bad guy mistakenly eats a whole bunch of drugs and watches Mrs. Brady's daisy-patterned dress take on life, for there was a caricature of a Peter Max poster, a return to lava-lamp luminescence. The movie's writer was hooting at narcotic-induced "visions."

It was the second time in six months that I'd seen this attitude in the theater. The first was when Alan Alda and Lily Tomlin were portrayed as LSD-producing sixties refugees still seeking their inner worlds through Leary-inspired technique in *Flirting with Disaster*. The culture is beginning to laugh at drug-induced stupor. Good.

What's not good is that it's not yet uniformly laughing at the substitute—New Age mysticism. And there remains a strong pull toward chemically assisted introspection. It's quick, and it's easy. People believe it's pleasurable, and perhaps it is. Of course, it's also fake.

Look. Give a dog some drugs, and the dog will experience visions. It's hardly communication with God. Why, then, are so many ready to believe that drug-assisted vision quests yield authentic spiritual experience?

I am inclined to believe testimony of mystical experiences when it is given by the soberest people around. If the very rigorous Chuck Colson were to take me aside to tell me of his "visions," I'd listen carefully. When Father Keating says, against the backdrop of his fifty-three years in monastic practice, that he had one "mystical" experience worth relating and it lasted a relatively short time, I want to learn about that. Authenticity fairly screams from such circumstances.

But they are rare. And the vision-blessed, like the rich, are different from you and me. You and I, well, we have orthodoxy. We have the forms. It's what God wanted us to have. We have Scripture. It is rich, complete, and filling. We may graduate someday to a different relationship with God that involves visions, and in the next life, we certainly will. But the odds are that we had better be prepared to experience an extraordinary God through some very ordinary means.

In the course of defending belief, a person of faith will be asked about the benefits of belief. Many who ask the question would like to hear that mystical bliss awaits. But the promise is just not available to the apologist, the evangelist, or the ordinary Christian. Belief does, indeed, have an emotional component, but its rational, intellectual side is just as crucial. You can promise the interested truth and wisdom. But you cannot promise visions and voices. That is New Age's pitch. That is New Age's trap.

This recognition should embolden the rank-and-file Christian. We are followers of Christ, not because it feels good—though it can. We are followers of Christ because His gospel is true.

Job's Exclusive

17

The television folks of my acquaintance—and I suspect this is a rule with only an occasional exception—are a fairly unchurched, non-believing group. When *Searching for God in America* got under way, a little joke sprang up around the hallways at KCET: "Did you interview God yet?"

I'd always reply that I was still working on an "exclusive," a television term for a one-of-a-kind interview with a newsmaker.

The idea of interviewing God is a pretty ridiculous one. Sure, the questions are easy enough to frame, but imagining the process borders on the absurd. Instead, I tried to make do by posing some of the most difficult questions of life to eminent theologians or religious leaders. The ability to defend one's own belief is greatly enhanced by listening to great theologians answer difficult questions.

I asked each of my guests the same question in slightly different ways. With some of the interviews, I asked it two, three, and even four times: Why was there such obvious suffering and pain in our days? Why did God allow it now? Why had He allowed it throughout history?

In the anthology portion of the book, I included the excerpt from the writings of philosopher George Santayana, which concluded that, "To remove an evil is not to remove the fact that it has existed. . . . The existence of any evil anywhere at any time absolutely ruins a total optimism."

To me, that is a powerful argument. Why would God allow suffering to enter into His creation? Why not a creation where the free will's choice was between good and best, not evil and good? Here are some of the responses I garnered:

CHUCK COLSON: I don't know. The only thing that I know is that I live in a sinful world, and the consequences of that sin are manifest in people. There is suffering, and inexplicable acts take place.

Why would a loving God allow this? Well, the only other choice for a loving God would be to control human nature, to take away our free will. He created us in the Garden, perfect. In Paradise. And then we sinned. Now we're living with the consequences of that sin. We feel them systemically, institutionally, in terms of disease and chaos. The Bible predicted that would be the case. But for everybody there is the possibility of ultimate redemption. I mean, that's all that really matters as you go through life. Maybe the rich young ruler you were referring to earlier had a harder time seeing that truth than a beggar like Lazarus did. Mother Teresa argues that the poor can see better. Through all their pain and suffering, they see the reality of God in a way that those of us who live comfortable, upper-middle-class lives cannot.

ROBERTA HESTENES: It's not that these issues are settled. I was standing in a famine camp in Ethiopia for the first time. And the shrouded bodies of babies were piled up shoulder height; they were just the babies who had died that day. And I was handed a child who looked to me to be about a year old, and I was told that the child was five but so severely malnourished that he would probably die. And we did, as Christians, go in there and save hundreds of thousands of lives because people cared.

On one level the question is, Why is there *goodness?* When you look at the world, it's a real question. Can you explain that? People tend to take goodness for granted. But if the world is self-created, or if we're all here just by some accidental happening, explain the goodness that we see, the love and care that are so real even if they're alongside evil.

As I walked in that camp, the mothers cried out to me—as mother to mother. And I noticed that every woman in that camp wore a cross around her neck. They were Christians. That country had been Christian from the earliest centuries. There are people who sometimes naively say that faith exempts us from participation in suffering, that faith is some kind of easy trip we make, that if we just accept Jesus we will be wealthy or successful or prosperous or things will be easy. But that's not what faith is about. Faith is a personal meeting with God in reality—in our brokenness, in the struggles that every one of us goes through, and in the midst of the evil that is out there.

But that reality also includes the beauty and the love and the other good things. And we could talk as long about the places where I've seen caring—where at the human level there was nothing in it for the people who cared. They gave themselves simply because they believed it was right. And that love was at the heart of the universe, and they were participating in that love. And I would have to say that so far in my journey, I have seen more of that good than I have of the other.

CECIL MURRAY: I don't think God causes the negative. I think that God says, "When you're sick of being sick, here I am. I told you what it takes to have your garden, but you want to live east of Eden. You don't want to live in Eden. You want to be your own god. Now where did it lead you? Even with your wars, you win the wars and then you lose them because the people you defeated are richer, wealthier, steadier, than you are. When are you going to stop hurting each other? When you're ready, here's a way, here's a formula." That's all God can do: "I stand at the door and knock. I can't knock your head off. I give you a certain amount of freedom to make a decision. Your bad decisions are killing you. Look at you."

HAROLD KUSHNER: But in terms of tragedy, I don't know. I can believe that goodness would not be possible without the possibility of evil. I can believe that if we were forced, if we were programmed, if we were hard-wired always to do the right thing, it would be neat, it would be nice, it would be convenient. But it wouldn't be good, because it wouldn't be a choice. That I can understand.

I'm not sure I understand disease. I'm not sure I understand genetic accidents. I'm not sure I understand the vulnerability. One can explain to me scientifically that if our bones were so strong that if we fell down they wouldn't break, they would also be too heavy for us to walk. And biologically that's satisfying; but there is a part of me that says, *You know, if I were God, I could have come up with a better solution.* So I'm stumped by that. I can't read God's mind. All I can deal with is the cards I'm dealt.

This is a world where human beings are vulnerable to crime, illness, injury. This is a world where people can as easily choose to be mean and vicious as they can choose to be good. In fact, sometimes it's easier to choose to be mean. There seems to be a kind of moral law of gravity that pulls us down—that makes it easier to lie than to tell the truth when the truth is embarrassing, that makes it easier to sleep late than to get up early, that makes it easier to be selfish than to be generous.

If I were creating the world, I might have done it differently. I might have looked at the results and thought, *You know, that was a mistake; it should have been the way God had it on the blueprint originally.* But I'm not involved in shaping the world. I'm only involved in dealing with it as I find it. I don't know why God made the world the way He did. I'm not prepared to say this is the best of all possible worlds. But this is the world we have. And I try to live in it.

THOMAS KEATING: To find this true happiness we have to be motivated out of our self-centeredness. And not only when we're cooperating with Him but through the trials and difficulties of life, it takes God a lot of time to get the message across that maybe our programs for happiness are not so hot. We may have to find ourselves in tragedy, in a terrible divorce, in a rehab center, before we begin to wonder whether our programs for happiness around power and affection, esteem and security, were really the right ones.

All of these are provocative replies. They reflect centuries-old thinking and centuries-old answers that are available to anyone intent on finding them.

I walked away directed by Rabbi Kushner to the Book of Job—to that chronicle of a man suffering mightily. If you are unfamiliar with it, it is critical to understand only that Satan suggested to God that everyone on earth would believe when all goes well and that none would believe when all goes bad. God replied that a certain man, Job, would remain faithful no matter what.

That was Job's bad luck, really, to have lived so righteously as to impress God Himself. Here's how God pointed out Job to Satan: "Have you considered my servant Job, that there is none like him on the earth, a blameless and upright man, who fears God and turns away from evil" (Job 1:8). Bad luck for Job, for prodded by Satan into testing Job, God sent every sort of trial: illness of the most horrific sorts, the death of children, the loss of wealth, and the nattering of friends.

Finally Job broke and demanded an answer from God. Job believed his treatment to be unjust. He listed out the details of his righteous life and demanded an answer: "Here is my signature! let the Almighty answer me!" (Job 31:35). And Job got an earful. Here is Scripture's account of God's answer to a man who was angered by unjust suffering:

> Then the LORD answered Job out of the whirlwind:
> "Who is this that darkens counsel by words without
> knowledge?
> Gird up your loins like a man,
> I will question you, and you shall declare to me.
>
> "Where were you when I laid the foundation of the
> earth?
> Tell me, if you have understanding.
> Who determined its measurements—surely you
> know!
> Or who stretched the line upon it?
> On what were its bases sunk,
> or who laid its cornerstone,
> when the morning stars sang together,
> and all the sons of God shouted for joy?
>
> "Or who shut in the sea with doors,
> when it burst forth from the womb;
> when I made the clouds its garment,
> and thick darkness its swaddling band,
> and prescribed bounds for it,
> and set bars and doors,
> and said, 'Thus far shall you come, and no farther,
> and here shall your proud waves be stayed'?
>
> "Have you commanded the morning since your days
> began,
> and caused the dawn to know its place,
> that it might take hold of the skirts of the earth,
> and the wicked be shaken out of it?
> It is changed like clay under a seal,

and it is dyed like a garment.
From the wicked their light is withheld,
   and their uplifted arm is broken.

"Have you entered into the springs of the sea,
   or walked in the recesses of the deep?
Have the gates of death been revealed to you,
   or have you seen the gates of deep darkness?
Have you comprehended the expanse of the earth?
   Declare, if you know all this.

"Where is the way to the dwelling of light,
   and where is the place of darkness,
that you may take it to its territory
   and that you may discern the paths to its home?
You know, for you were born then,
   and the number of your days is great!
"Have you entered the storehouses of the snow,
   or have you seen the storehouses of the hail,
which I have reserved for the time of trouble,
   for the day of battle and war?
What is the way to the place where the light is
     distributed,
   or where the east wind is scattered upon the earth?

"Who has cleft a channel for the torrents of rain,
   and a way for the thunderbolt,
to bring rain on a land where no man is,
   on the desert in which there is no man;
to satisfy the waste and desolate land,
   and to make the ground put forth grass?

"Has the rain a father,
   or who has begotten the drops of dew?
From whose womb did the ice come forth,
   and who has given birth to the hoarfrost of heaven?
The waters become hard like stone,

> *and the face of the deep is frozen.*
> *"Can you bind the chains of the Pleiades,*
> *   or loose the cords of Orion?*
> *Can you lead forth the Mazzaroth in their season,*
> *   or can you guide the Bear with its children?*
> *Do you know the ordinances of the heavens?*
> *   Can you establish their rule on the earth?" (Job 38:1–33)*

Not really satisfactory, is it? This excerpt from a lengthy speech by God—an extended shout, really—is, however, fundamentally thrilling and scary, an awe-inspiring display of celestial authority, a rebuke that has echoed across thousands of years and rings in ears even today. Many scholars believe this is the oldest book in the Bible. Certainly it addresses one of the oldest questions in the universe: Why me?

Scholars, not just scribblers like me, have been wrestling with God's response for millennia. I like Job's response to His thunder from the whirlwind. It was complete submission to the immensity of the God he had just encountered. Here is Job's quiet reply:

> *I know that thou canst do all things,*
> *   and that no purpose of thine can be thwarted.*
> *"Who is this that hides counsel without knowledge?"*
> *Therefore I have uttered what I did not understand,*
> *   things too wonderful for me, which I did not know.*
> *   (Job 42:1–3)*

All the modern thinkers I interviewed, all the anthology selections I edited, cannot approach in completeness this final response by a righteous man hard-pressed by events. It is not an "answer," of course, not a fully formed "proof." It is, however, sufficient.

As Harold Kushner told me, "He would be a pretty puny God if I could understand Him."

And the God of the whirlwind is an infinite opposite of small.

18

Would You Earn a Bible?

The defense of belief may not require great courage. I've argued as much. And there are certainly answers to the most difficult theological questions available from authorities as old as Job or as newly arrived as the youngest pastor in town. But more than eagerness to engage is required if mockery and contempt are to be routed and disbelievers moved at least a bit toward tolerance. Knowledge is required. At least a little bit.

In my church in California, the third grade is a year of particular focus for the Sunday school program. The church targets its eight- and nine-year-olds for initial instruction in the basics of Christian belief.

And "basics" means exactly that: The foundation stones are laid in this year. Prior to third grade there is a gentle and very unsystematic approach, emphasizing simple songs and ageless Bible stories. In grades four and above, there is a focus on particular books of Scripture. Third grade is the boot camp of Christian belief.

September marks the beginning of this basic training. It wraps up in June. Those students who can "master" the material "earn" their Bible.

Now, here's the embarrassing part—the complete "Third Grade Checklist to Earn a Bible for Graduation":

❑ **Recite the books of the New Testament.** (November–March)

Matthew	1 Corinthians	1 Thessalonians
Mark	2 Corinthians	2 Thessalonians
Luke	Galatians	1 Timothy
John	Ephesians	2 Timothy
Acts	Philippians	Titus
Romans	Colossians	Philemon

Hebrews	2 Peter	3 John
James	1 John	Jude
1 Peter	2 John	Revelation

❑ **Sing the Doxology from memory.** (November)
Praise God from whom all blessings flow
Praise Him all creatures here below
Praise Him above, ye heavenly host
Praise Father, Son, and Holy Ghost.

❑ **Demonstrate passing the peace of Christ.** (April)
Say: "May the peace of Christ be with you!"
Respond: "And with you."

❑ **Recite the Lord's Prayer.** (November)

❑ **Recite John 3:16.** (March/April/May)
"For God so loved the world that he gave his only Son, that whoever believes in him should not perish but have eternal life."

❑ **Recite Romans 3:23.** (October/November)
"All have sinned and fall short of the glory of God."

❑ **Recite 1 John 1:9** (December/January/February)
"If we confess our sins, he is faithful and just, and will forgive our sins and cleanse us from all unrighteousness."

❑ **Identify pictures of:** (September)
Pulpit, pew, font, and Communion table.

❑ **State a simple explanation of baptism.** (March)

❑ **State a simple explanation of Communion.** (September/October)

❑ **State a simple explanation of the symbolism of bread and wine in Communion.** (September)

❑ **State in order the liturgical (church) year.** (May)
Advent, Christmas, Epiphany, Lent, Holy Week, Easter, and Pentecost.

❑ **Find a hymn by number in the hymnal.** (October)

❑ **Find in the Bible: Genesis, Psalms, and Matthew.** (October)

❑ **Additional items for third-graders to learn:**
Demonstrate the responses, "We lift our prayer to you . . ."
"Hear our prayer, O Lord."

❑ **State the correct order of worship:**
Prelude, call to worship, praise, confession, sermon, prayers of the people, passing the peace of Christ, offering, and benediction.

❑ **Identify the pastor by picture.**

❑ **Write: A simple call to worship**
A simple prayer of thanksgiving and praise
A simple prayer of confession

That's it, the entire third-grade curriculum. Now it's time to divide our class into believers, bystanders, and bad guys.

It is difficult to imagine many bad guys *buying* this book, though I certainly hope it will be given to many of them. Who they are and why they are so categorized comes later.

The crucial distinction at this point is the difference between a believer and a bystander. Bystanders will think this distinction is subtle and nuanced. It's not. Believers already understand it.

Bystanders will want to understand themselves to be believers and will bridle at any other categorization. But however discomforting it may be, bystanders will quickly recognize themselves as such if there is any openness at all.

Here are a few guidelines. They are not absolute. But they are generally reliable.

Believers attend church services on a *very* regular basis. It is unusual for them not to be there.

Bystanders attend either occasionally, infrequently, or not at all.

Believers teach their children and others' children the essentials of the faith. Bystanders entrust that chore to others.

Believers have witnessed to their faith, even if they find it unpleasant. Bystanders are theoretically willing to do so if approached but have never been approached.

Believers read Scripture even though it's a chore. Bystanders intend to get around to it.

Believers honor the men and women in the leadership of the church. Bystanders, when they notice the church leaders at all, are consistent only in their willingness to critique.

No job is beneath a believer. Bystanders don't want many jobs but can sacrifice themselves for leadership positions if coaxed and pleaded with.

Believers are full of God's forgiveness and love. Bystanders know the rules.

Believers savor and seek more and more teaching about God. Bystanders have what they need and would rather not be bothered.

This is a harsh exercise. I do not enjoy it. Nothing so identifies an American of a certain class, background, and education as his or her absolute fear of being thought judgmental or intolerant, and I'm in that group. It's almost ludicrous, in fact, to see how ordinary, intelligent people will flee from the prospect of condemning or even raising questions about another's behavior.

That reticence is actually a very refined form of cowardice, a fear of losing prestige or friendship. It is also a retreat from a basic, God-given need to be judged and evaluated, scolded or praised.

Here's Rabbi Harold Kushner on this subject:

Let me tell you a story . . . I saw it many years ago on television. A story of a man who dies and wakes up a moment later at the end of a long line. At the front of the line he sees two doors—one marked heaven and one marked hell. And there's an usher, and the usher says, "Move along, keep the line moving. Choose either door, heaven or hell, and walk in."

The man says to the usher, "What happened to the Last Judgment?

Where are my deeds weighed and measured? Where am I told if I am a good person or a bad person?" The usher says, "You know, I don't know where that story ever got started. We don't do that here. We've never done it. We don't have the staff to do that here. I mean, look, ten thousand people arrive every minute. I'm supposed to sit down with every one and go over his whole life? We'd never get anywhere. Now, choose either door. Choose heaven or hell, and go in. I don't want to see you again."

And in the television sketch the man walks through the door marked hell. As I understand that, he makes that choice not because he thinks he's a bad person who wants to be punished, but because he believes he's a human being who wants to be judged. I think there is a human, fundamental need to be taken seriously as a moral agent. We need to believe that the universe cares if we are good or bad, if we are truthful or deceitful, if we are faithful or betraying our vows.

You know what it's like, Hugh? Can you remember when you were in college and you stayed up all Sunday night trying to finish a paper because you really wanted to be good? And you handed it in at ten o'clock Monday morning and you got it back at ten o'clock Wednesday morning with a little pencil check next to your name and nothing else on the paper? Clearly the professor never bothered to read it; he just gave you credit for doing it. How did you feel? You felt cheated. Why should you knock yourself out if nobody cares?

The ultimate challenge to a human being, I think, is that question: Why should we go to the trouble of being good if nobody cares? And that's why I must believe, not only that God exists and not only that God replenishes the love, strength, and courage of human beings, but that God cares how we live. God cares how I earn and spend my money. God cares who I sleep with. God cares what kind of language I use. Because unless I believe that God cares, I don't feel that I am being taken seriously as a moral agent. That's where the need to believe in a moral agent, I think, comes from.

The renewal of the Christian church is tied in part to the willingness of Christians everywhere to examine critically their own behavior and the behavior of their churches, denominations, and the entire church as a whole. The damage done by decades of go-along-to-get-along in the culture at large has also taken a toll on the church so that there is a widespread paralysis when it comes to judgment.

Here's a sample of "judgment": If you cannot pass the Third Graders Checklist, chances are you are a bystander. And you're a mess. God exists, and He cares if you care if He exists. Your indifference to basics may be ticking Him off.

That statement will anger many, many people. It's judgmental. It's intolerant. Its message carries an implicit condemnation of many fellow Christians.

But compare the implications of an inability to pass this third grade test with the implications of an inability to pass other tests geared to eight and nine-year-olds.

If you can't read at a third-grade level, are you genuinely literate?

If you can't add, subtract, and multiply at a third-grade level, can you properly be thought to know even basic math?

If your manners are at the level of an average young boy or girl, can you be thought civilized?

Would you be complacent about a level of learning in any subject if that level was deemed to be at grade three?

No doubt the lack of urgency to know the essentials of faith can be traced to the simplicity of Christ's message: "I am the way, and the truth, and the life; no one comes to the Father, but by me" (John 14:6). It is a message and a salvation available to simple people.

But it is not true that those who have received the simple message, and thus the Lord, need themselves be simple.

Bystanders find that idea seductive. "I've accepted Jesus. I'm saved. I don't read theology." I defer to C. S. Lewis:

> Theology is like a map. . . . But that map is based on the experience of hundreds of people who really were in touch with God—experiences compared with which any thrills or pious feelings you and I are likely to get on our own are very elementary and very confused.

And where Lewis left off underscoring the need for theology, I add the crucial need to learn church history. Theology is the premise for understanding church history, but we need both.

Not so long ago the dual need for theology and church history was assumed. But the church has been dumbed down. And the church has suffered for it.

An example. In my travels over the past year and especially in my media interviews, a frequent objection to the *idea* of religious belief—not any particular belief but all or any of them—was that belief provoked bloodshed.

An individual conversant with even broad outlines of church history can deal with such objections. Here's an exchange I had with Pastor Roberta Hestenes:

HUGH HEWITT: You yourself are a Presbyterian. Presbyterianism is an outgrowth of John Calvin's teaching, and he was not the world's least-severe person in his faith.

ROBERTA HESTENES: He was serious. I don't know that *severe* is a fair word.

HUGH HEWITT: Well, people died in his time because of a failure to commit to a particular doctrine. Does that make you at all uncomfortable with the Presbyterian tradition?

ROBERTA HESTENES: Well, first, let's do our history. Only one person died—

HUGH HEWITT: Who was that person?

ROBERTA HESTENES: Servetus. In Geneva. And I wish that he hadn't died.

Second, there were religious wars in the next century; they were following the Reformation and later. I think people often take the Crusades, the religious wars, and they put them all together as if that was the total reality. But they're looking at a fairly small slice of history.

The danger in American Christianity today, by and large, is not that we are too severe with our faith, but that we've watered it down so that it is hard to distinguish our faith from the secular culture around us. And my own belief is that the danger in American faith is not hellfire-and-brimstone preaching. When I hear people talking about being in reaction to hellfire and brimstone, I say, "When was the last time you really heard a sermon or a message of that type?" In the last decade, American

Christians have so emphasized the love of God that we have sometimes forgotten the holiness of God. I think the Scripture shows us both faces, so to speak, of God.

Hestenes's dismissal of the conventional wisdom regarding Calvin was delivered with an authority that knowledge bestows. She then moved quickly to put religious-inspired bloodshed of that day into its context: "a fairly small slice of history." Disbelievers will object that she is too dismissive—what about the Huguenots!—but absolute numbers matter, and the comparative carnage of such secular evils as the Nazis' death camps, the Soviet-imposed famine, or Pol Pot's regime quickly end the conversation.

But only if the believer is equipped to argue the case. Only if the believer is not a bystander.

In order to advance the truth, people must know it. Possess it. Understand it.

It is not enough to know that personal salvation is yours. That knowledge compels additional learning. And that learning begins with the basics.

19

Apologetics Does Not Mean the Science of Saying You're Sorry

Christian apologetics is the branch of theology devoted to persuading skeptics of the truth of the gospel. "Apologetics," wrote scholar Mortimer Adler, "is the effort on the part of a person of a given religious faith to argue for its exclusive or superior possession of the truth as against all other competing faiths."

The foremost Christian apologist of this century is the Englishman C. S. Lewis, who earned that position by virtue of the massive distribution of his works and the uncommon ability of his writings to teach and touch people. When I am suggesting readings to either the interested or the newly converted, I always suggest Lewis's *Mere Christianity* and *The Screwtape Letters.* The former is a primer on basic Christian theology, the latter a literary romp that amuses even as it instructs us in crucial lessons.

Apologetics makes the difficult accessible. It is the art of using commonplace language and construction to reveal the persuasiveness of the gospel.

The greatest teachers are apologists. In my interview work I have run into great examples of apologetics practiced by modern masters. Here is Chuck Colson using one question of mine to present an entire argument on the truthfulness of the gospel, an argument that is quite attractive:

HUGH HEWITT: A couple of times you've commented in your writings and in your speeches that Watergate and its unraveling convinced you of the factual accuracy of the resurrection of Christ. How so?

CHUCK COLSON: Well, it's a great analogy, actually. If anybody really looks at what happened in Watergate, they would discover that Nixon did not know the full scope of the Watergate cover-up until March 21. John Dean, his counsel, paraded into the office and said, "Mr. President, there's a cancer growing on your presidency." And if you look at the tape of that day, you'll see that was when he laid out everything that had gone on, and Nixon suddenly knew there was a criminal cover-up. Haldeman called me a couple of days later. I did not know about that meeting, but he told me some things. And I said, "Bob, you'd better get a lawyer." I think everybody at that point knew that it was serious and that the White House was involved.

John Dean went off to Camp David to write a report, began to think that he was in trouble. And he wrote in his own memoirs with refreshing candor that on April 4, less than three weeks later, he went to the prosecutors to make a deal, as he put it, to save his own skin. The moment he did that, Jeb Magruder went to the prosecutors. And a whole string of guys went to the prosecutors. I took a lie detector test. Here we were, the twelve most powerful men in the world. We were surrounding the president of the United States. And we wouldn't keep a lie for three weeks!

The truth of the gospel depends upon the fact that Jesus Christ was bodily raised from the dead. How do we know that? We have the eyewitness testimony of five hundred people, according to the apostle Paul. We have eleven apostles who were with Him and who saw Him raised from the dead. There was Thomas, who put his finger in the wound because he doubted Jesus. And all of the apostles were with Jesus after He was bodily resurrected from the tomb. Now, if He was bodily resurrected, that is the most convincing evidence of the divinity of Jesus Christ. And there's the testimony of the apostles for forty years. And they had no power like we did in Watergate. They were persecuted. They were crucified upside down. All but one died a martyr's death. They were stoned, beaten, and not once did they deny that they had seen Christ risen from the dead.

I believe that men will give their lives for something they believe to be true. They will never give their lives for something they know to be false. If Christ hadn't risen, the apostle Peter would have been just like John Dean. He would have gone and turned state's evidence to save his own skin. Not one of them denied the resurrection of Christ, which to me means that they had to have seen the risen Christ, God in the flesh.

Otherwise they would have saved their own skins just like we did in Watergate.

Apologetics requires facility with the language of the current culture, for the archaic cannot be persuasive. Thus the power of Colson's example, drawing as it does on a relatively recent burst of history—Watergate—and using it by comparison to the incredible attachment to the good news exhibited by the apostles.

Every generation produces good apologists. Inevitably the best are scholars. They are competent at making the apparently extra-rational persuasive. They can often provide the bridge for a skeptic unsettled by what must always remain an awesome leap of faith.

So too does theology function in this fashion, and not just its branch of apologetics. I repeat again my excerpt from Lewis earlier: "Theology is like a map. . . . That map is based on the experience of hundreds of people who really were in touch with God—experiences compared with which any thrills or pious feelings you or I are likely to get on our own are very elementary and very confused." In other words, Christians at the end of the millennium do not have to reinvent the wheel. Even the most tentative Christian has available to him or her thousands of pages of persuasive arguments. The faith can be defended quite vigorously using replies and explanations that have stood the test of many years and many skeptics.

Unfortunately, we've abandoned knowledge standards in the culture to such an extent that the language of theology and the knowledge of past apologetics is beyond the grasp of vast numbers of Americans. Theology was not intended for the seminaries. Apologetics certainly wasn't. Both were intended for all believers. But their fall into desuetude is so complete that the recapturing of theology and apologetics requires a major effort.

Two examples help illustrate how much Christians have collectively forgotten. Both are again drawn from the Chuck Colson interview. In my conversation with him, Colson referenced Pascal's wager, and we both referenced Saint Augustine's pears. These are two-word descriptive summaries of vitally important theological arguments. Among our television audience, even though it was a PBS audience, there were thousands of people for whom those shorthand phrases carried no reference at all.

Here from Saint Augustine's *Confessions,* is the brief version of Augustine's pears:

> There was a pear-tree near our vineyard, loaded with fruit that was attractive neither to look at nor to taste. Late one night a band of ruffians, myself included, went off to shake down the fruit and carry it away; for we had continued our games out of doors until well after dark, as was our pernicious habit. We took away an enormous quantity of pears, not to eat them ourselves, but simply to throw them to the pigs. Perhaps we ate some of them, but our real pleasure consisted in doing something that was forbidden. . . . As it was not the fruit that gave me pleasure, I must have got it from the crime itself, from the thrill of having partners in sin.

Augustine's theft of the pears, unprovoked and unnecessary, is a famous example of the essential nature of man—an evil one. To speak of Augustine's pears is to reference the theological understanding that man is not basically good, but that man is essentially bad. And not just bad, evil. It is also to reference Augustine's apologetic technique and one of his classics, *The Confessions.*

Pascal's wager, or his "great gamble," is more difficult to convey. Blaise Pascal was a great French mathematician and philosopher from the early 1600s. To summarize the "wager" put forward by Pascal, British historian Paul Johnson states simply that, "Pascal argued that Christianity provided a better answer than a solution which depended purely on reason. In all probability, it was a better bet."

Colson translated Pascal to mean that skeptics ought to believe because, "You've got nothing to lose. It's almost Pascal's wager theory. If I'm right, then [Christianity] is the greatest news you will ever learn." I have always understood Pascal's wager to mean that belief cannot possibly hurt you, but disbelief—if there is a God who punishes disbelief—can result in an eternal punishment, and thus the better bet is belief.

The exact phrasing of Pascal's gamble or the significance of Augustine's pears is not the issue. The only issue is the culture's deafness to such allusions. I would welcome an objection from an audience that I had wrongly described Pascal's wager or that I had shorted Augustine's own reflections on the pears he stole. Unless I present these allusions in a seminary or a school of philosophy, however, I am unlikely to encounter an objection at all. In fact, I'm likely to encounter blank faces.

I teach constitutional law in a new law school at an old university, Chapman University. In the fall of 1996, my evening-division class consisted of approximately eighty students who were bright and highly motivated. The vast majority were working already and were pursuing law degrees as a second career or as a way to enhance their abilities in their present jobs. They are superb and talented students with great educations and real-world accomplishments.

And not one of them recognized Augustine's pears or Pascal's wager.

I suspect a survey of Harvard, Yale, and Stanford Law School classes would yield the same result. Certainly there was no discussion of such matters in the early '80s at the University of Michigan Law School—my alma mater. This silence on theological basics is no doubt replicated in all graduate programs and probably undergraduate programs as well.

John Agresto is the charismatic, indeed irrepressible, president of St. John's College in Santa Fe, New Mexico—the "Great Books" school. It's fun to throw a "pop quiz" for a college president, so I asked John to define both concepts, which he nearly carried off with complete accuracy, naming the *Confessions* but missing the exact story. Agresto shares with me my belief that most undergraduates would totally fail the same quiz in astonishing numbers. In fact, colleges like St. John's that continue to insist that *all* of its students read such things are rapidly becoming the monasteries of this century—the places where learning endures in the face of the widespread moral illiteracy outside the walls of the campus.

The general collapse of moral literacy provides the challenge to modern apologists, as well as evangelists. And is one of the great explanations for the phenomenon of millions of people who are embarrassed by Christian belief. Apologists especially must recognize that they are working against the backdrop of a popular culture that has not merely systematically undermined attention span but one that has pulverized common concepts and common learning. There is no legacy of theological learning that can be presumed. It is all gone, as completely destroyed as the study of Latin. (In fact, Latin—making a small come-back—is better off than theology.) This scattering of accumulated knowledge has left two generations of Christians aware only of how little they know when it comes to defending what they know to be the truth.

The church has been an accomplice in this march toward theological incoherence. Examine any widely popular elementary Sunday school curriculum, and while abundant Scripture lessons and some Bible memorization are no doubt there, there will be a disproportionate attention to crafts—to keeping students quiet and amused. The effort to educate has been minimized as part of the church's rolling surrender to the culture.

Here's the problem. Nature abhors a vacuum, and young minds abhor vacuity. If theology does not fill the mind, New Age silliness will. Teachers and churches face a daunting task—they must work harder to make doctrine interesting and against longer odds than ever, but they cannot give up!

If the language of moral decision-making is lost, it must be reclaimed. If the Sunday schools are stuck with trashy outlines and silly lessons, then Sunday school teachers must revolt.

It's not easy, and it's not exciting. It is only necessary and urgent.

At the level of the pulpit as well, pastor and preacher must demand more of their audiences. It is a *teaching* job, not a therapy session.

The initial burst of energy in the church at large that exploded in the early '90s will not be sustained without this deepening of knowledge. As the subject of theology is God, then theology is compelled to be interesting. It cannot be dull or cannot remain dead even in untalented hands. It is ominous only from a distance.

In the anthology portion of the book *Searching for God in America,* I included the Roman Catholic "Baltimore Catechism." I did so because it is an old friend to millions of Americans, a reassuring memory from a more predictable and certain time. I had grown up with a generation of teachers who could recite long excerpts from the Baltimore Catechism. That shared certainty of both what was believed and why gave confidence to the postwar generation of Catholic lay-readership that powered the Catholic Church up to Vatican II.

Had my book been open to writings from other countries, I would have included the short Westminster Catechism. It's not easily available, but for Protestants it can serve the same purpose as did the Baltimore Catechism for Catholics—a lengthy reminder of the essentials of religious belief. From that foundation can come marvelous apologetics geared for the next millennium. There are other catechisms, and there are even more accessible summaries of key doctrines and crucial apologetic arguments.

Beyond catechisms, there are a half-dozen classics of Christian theology that all believers should have seen at some point. There are hundreds of excellent Christian bookstores in the United States, and most of the major secular stores have begun to expand their religion sections. Each year publishers reissue classics and introduce new offerings. The elite media hardly ever review a book that treats orthodox belief with respect and seeks to expound it. Just because these offerings are not noticed by the secular press does not mean they do not exist. But effort is required.

The believer convinced of the need to move beyond his or her habits would be well served to subscribe to *Christianity Today* or *Moody's, New Man,* or *World.* Each of these magazines approaches the world from an evangelical's view. They all provide some guideposts to the booksellers. The assists are in place. They need only be used.

It is a marvelous encouragement to Embarrassed Believers to discover both vertical and horizontal allies. The vertical allies are the generations of believers—twenty centuries' worth—who have gone before him or her. The horizontal allies comprise the fellowship of all believers now living, many of whom have organized the materials and the means to defend the faith. It is not a lonely battle. In fact, it is the largest force on the planet.

On April 18, 1944—the height of World War II, more than two months prior to D-Day—C. S. Lewis made an appearance at the head office of Electric and Musical Industries, Ltd. to answer questions from a diverse audience including believers and nonbelievers. The entire exchange is reprinted in *God in the Dock* and *The Grand Miracle*. In rereading the exchange, which must have lasted about an hour, I came to see what it was about Lewis that allowed him to accomplish what he did, and what it is about him that, more than thirty years after his death, still inspires Christians by the millions and tens of millions .

Confidence.

Lewis waded into an audience some of whose members were—judging from their questions—hostile to his project, and he efficiently and apparently effortlessly dispatched every query. He did so with great good humor and an impossible-to-deny intelligence.

He was in command of the field. A man to be admired.

David Beers is a young writer whom I interviewed in the fall of 1996 about his then-new book, *Blue Sky Dream,* a fine memoir about growing up in a defense-industry family in West San Jose in the '50s, '60s, and '70s. Some of Beers's politics are wildly different from mine, but he has a knack for a good descriptive phrase. One of those described an exchange he overheard between his father, an accomplished pilot, and a control-tower operator. He described the exchange as, "the way men must speak to each other when they know exactly what they are doing." There is such a style of speaking, and it is not limited to pilots and air traffic controllers. In fact, it is a style that appears in all fields inhabited by superior skill.

Lewis had this confidence, the ability to talk (and write), "the way men must speak to each other when they know exactly what they are doing."

And Christians hobbled by a lack of training, or a lack of eloquence, stand back and read Lewis with an admiration born of envy but tempered by pride in sharing in the same enterprise.

It is thrilling to watch Lewis work in the same way it was thrilling to watch Muhammad Ali fight or John Elway control the last three minutes of a game (a very difficult admission for me, a die-hard Browns fan who waits for the return of Lake Erie football in the fall of 1999). When Will Smith starred as the fighter pilot in the movie *Independence Day,* theater-goers rallied to his character, not because of his braggadocio, but because it was backed up with a war-fighting skill that though completely fictional was nevertheless a very pleasant imagining.

Here's an example of Lewis in form: At the appearance before the head office of Electric and Musical Industries, Ltd., an unidentified voice attempted to trap Lewis in one of the ancient doctrinal controversies. The "voice" in the crowd did not pose a question but rather asserted a position. It is common for speakers to endure lectures from audience members invited to pose questions. I doubt if I have given a speech in the last five years where such an individual has not appeared. Here's how Lewis responded:

> VOICE: We don't qualify to heaven by practice, but salvation is obtained at the Cross. We do nothing to obtain it, but follow Christ. We may have pain or tribulation, but nothing we do qualifies us for heaven, but Christ.

> LEWIS: The controversy about faith and works is one that has gone on for a very long time, and it is a highly technical matter. I personally rely on the paradoxical text: "Work out your own salvation; for it is God [which] worketh in you" [Philippians 2:12 KJV]. It looks as if in one sense we do nothing, and in another case we do a damned lot. "Work out your own salvation in fear and troublings," but you must have it in you before you can work it out. But I have no wish to go further into it, as it would interest no one but the Christians present, would it?

Lewis's answer-that-was-not-an-answer was actually a rebuke. Let me paraphrase his response: "Here I am with an audience of nonbelievers, and you have posed a 'question' that has absorbed theologians for centuries. It has done so because it is one of the essential doctrines of faith to believe that faith in Christ is all that is needed for salvation—grace alone—but the primary author of that doctrine, Saint Paul writing in the epistle to the Romans, wrote elsewhere in ways suggesting the need for Christians to do good works. This tension in the primary authority has resulted in centuries of debate and even schism. Yet you bring it up in a forum in which there could not possibly be enough time to discuss the controversy, and you do so even as the opportunity slips away to interest nonbelievers in the efficacy and truth of belief. Shame on you."

My rephrasing is in fact longer than Lewis's original, underscoring Lewis's economy of argument, which reinforced its effectiveness.

Lewis's brilliance was not limited to the questions-and-answers form. In his essays, in his memoir, in his science fiction, in his children's literature, this quality of brilliance combined with a steady, matter-of-fact confidence in the truth of his message is what powers his appeal even now. (If there is a parent reading this chapter who has not read the seven books that comprise the *Chronicles of Narnia* aloud to his or her children, I hope you will begin tonight to do so, even at the expense of this and all other books except Scripture. Narnia is full of God's magic and can arm a child against much of the chaos that is coming her or his way. You owe it to your children to do this for them.)

It is unfortunately true that we also have encountered other teachers without Lewis's gifts, and the damage they have done is widespread.

I do not mean preachers who sin. Lewis sinned as well. We all do. It is not hypocrisy for Christians to sin. It's proof.

No, I'm referring to Christians who purport to represent "the church" and who teach in the name of God but do so badly, or so awkwardly that they allow, by force of their dismal performances, the impression to take root that theology is for the stupid and the narrow-minded or worse, that prolonged theological study makes one stupid or narrow-minded or worse.

God's gift of salvation is available to the simple, but God is not simple. Human history's most talented intellects are but idiots relative to the mind of God, so it is difficult to explain God to the world to begin with. We thus cannot allow the church to be slandered by the inarticulate or the anti-rational among its members.

Most will agree. So what to do?

In considering this problem, I've tried to keep in mind the fact that so many commentators are hand wringers and finger pointers. Secular column after column is stuffed full of often witty, sometimes scathing, attacks on some poor public official or political figure blundering about in the middle of an intractable mess of double dilemmas and triple conundrums. I have sat on the sidelines safe in my studio for six seasons, far removed from actual responsibility, and I know it's easy to throw darts. It's very, very difficult, on the other hand, to suggest even a passably coherent solution. Someday I hope this will be demonstrated on a *Meet the Press* show when a guest under fire turns the tables on host Tim Russert and asks, "Well, Tim, you've been doing this show for a decade. You must have picked up something. What would *you* do?" Russert would go to commercial, no doubt, and change guests.

So having blasted away at the theological and moral illiteracy of church leaders and followers alike, here's what I would do.

First, I'd ask every senior pastor to preach a long series on what theology is, who the great theologians are, and what crucial works should be read. Throughout this book, there are references to great writers and writings, but doctrinal differences preclude publishing a single comprehensive list. Each pastor ought to have a library full of classics to recommend to that particular congregation via a few, well-preached messages.

At the conclusion of that sermon series, I'd ask the pastors to request that small-group ministries undertake the study of at least one classic of theology.

Finally, I'd offer a Sunday school course as a midweek class on church history, and I hope the pastor obliges the congregation's very best teacher to lead that class.

After a year, the congregation would be ready to attempt some restructuring for their children's Sunday school classes so that long-term rehabilitation of the moral sense could begin.

This first step in the project is so simple that it might strike people as insufficient to the illness of Christian anti-intellectualism and theological and moral illiteracy. And it's not a cure. The prevailing model of the church as a therapy provider, not as the theological leader, is deeply ingrained; and it is indeed necessary to care for the millions wounded by this culture. Even as its refurbishing as an intellectual force gets under way, it cannot abandon its vast mission to the injured and the ailing.

But the prospects of success of a new Reformation in moral teaching must in reality be brighter than those confronting Luther in the Diet of Worms in 1521 when all the temporal power of the world gathered around him and the emperor and his fellow princes demanded he recant. Luther replied, "Since your Imperial Majesty and Lordships demand a simple answer, I will do so without horns or teeth as follows: Unless I am convicted by the testimony of scripture or by evident reason (for I trust neither in popes nor in councils alone, since it is obvious that they have often erred and contradicted themselves), I am convicted by the scripture which I have mentioned; and my conscience is captive to the Word of God. Therefore I cannot and will not recant, since it is difficult, unprofitable, and dangerous indeed to do anything against one's conscience. God help me. Amen."

Luther repaired to the relative safety of his own region shortly after declaring this theological stubbornness, but the courage he displayed has inspired the persecuted for more than four centuries. If a single monk could launch such a change, as Luther did, then of course the tools that modernity offers to the church are sufficient to the church's reclaiming its role as moral and intellectual leader.

Outside of the church, though, the need for restoring moral literacy is even more pressing. The therapeutic church is usually faithful to Scripture, and Scripture is the complete moral guide; the culture is so far separated from Scripture, though, that some organizations have taken to awarding prizes to secular writers who manage to use a biblical quotation in the course of a piece. Those prizes, while conceived with a noble purpose, are an indictment of the pathetic defense of the truth that has been on display for the past two generations.

Even as churches train members, and especially leaders, in moral theology and apologetics, those receiving that education must be preparing themselves to use that knowledge. I began this chapter with a description of one Lewis speech to a mixed audience. Today's leaders in every community have got to argue in all forums from explicitly moral premises. Unless argument is based on appeals to eternal and natural laws—to absolutes—then one argument is just as good as another.

Let me illustrate. Ozone depletion is a problem. It could be controlled in any number of ways. One way—very complicated, very technical—is to reduce gradually the ozone-depleting emissions of modern industrial operations. Another way is to murder every second child born in the world, thus decreasing demand for goods the production of which results in ozone-depleting emissions.

The latter proposal strikes most people as horrific, terrible, inhuman—yes, immoral. A debater on this issue could appeal to the fact that the act of murdering a child is unambiguously evil and is therefore not an acceptable solution under any circumstance.

It is harder to articulate *why* the act is immoral without reference to God's commandments, but the question is so infrequently asked that we need not worry about it yet. A debater would simply dismiss the proposal as immoral and move on.

As the plague of moral illiteracy has spread, it has become more and more difficult to make such appeals except in the most unambiguous circumstances such as the extreme one I just outlined. Here's an example of how confused the culture has become.

Searching for God in America generated enough interest after its initial broadcast and the book's release that media interviews continued to be scheduled well into the late summer and fall, even though the series concluded in July. One of those interviews was with with Bill Handel, Los Angeles's highest-rated morning talk-show host, on KFI-AM 640. Bill and I are old friends from our days on Saturday morning radio together, so we have an easy familiarity on the air that allows for our conversation to be completely spontaneous—which makes for the best radio.

Bill is quite the provocateur, known in California circles for a number of particularly controversial shows and positions. Though he is an educated and eloquent fellow, he's not above the coarse or bathroom humor-driven show. He can and does offend. One example was his "Handel's Bible Study," when he spent many weeks simply mocking the Book of Genesis.

I was scheduled for a Friday morning at 7:30 A.M., and it turned out to be the Friday following the Thursday on which President Clinton delivered his acceptance speech to the Democratic Convention in Chicago. Of course, this was also the day after the president's friend and closest political advisor, Dick Morris, resigned his post as chief campaign strategist after his relationship with a prostitute was reported, first in the tabloid press and then in the elite media.

Very quickly the conversation between Handel and me turned to Morris and his conduct. When I stated that, although Morris's conduct was evil, it would have little, if any, effect on the president's re-election, Handel was much more interested in my judgment of Morris than my political prognostication. He objected in strenuous terms: "The Holocaust is evil. Hitler is evil. A relationship with a prostitute isn't evil!" Bill was shouting, but since he almost always shouts, the audience probably did not sense the real disbelief his face showed. I'd used the "E" word on the airwaves, and he was shocked.

Handel's response illustrates the problem quite nicely. The Holocaust was evil; on that, all people can agree. But Handel assumed, as do quite a few people, that unless an act is *that* evil, then it's not deserving of the term.

Where, exactly, is the dividing line? Between evil and bad, I mean, between evil and tacky or low rent?

Almost everyone would agree that Morris's behavior was somehow "wrong." But since we lack the language of moral argument, we don't really name it evil, because that might somehow be over the top. And if cavorting with a prostitute—a not very rare occurrence—is not mere bad judgment but is evil, then aren't a lot of things evil? And if many routine things are evil, perhaps we are all evil and ought to consider seriously the implications of that evil.

I will return to Sunday school classes in a moment, so please stick with me a while longer.

An eight-year-old pushes his five-year-old brother for the fun of it, and the five-year-old falls and feels a passing hurt. Was this an evil act by the eight-year-old? You want to say no, because it happens all the time and the intent was only to discomfort, not to injure permanently.

An eight-year-old tortures and eventually drops a five-year-old to his death from a high-rise window because the younger child would not assist in a crime. An evil act? I can hear you say yes, of course.

Now what distinguishes the two acts? Degree of harm inflicted and severity of punishment, yes. But if both intended injury and suffering, are both eight-year-olds evil?

Both eight-year-olds have done wrong. Both are evil. We will punish them differently, but it serves no good purpose to deny that what motivated the first child is different only in degree from what motivated the second. Both eight-year-olds acted with the intent to injure while eliciting fear. The intent is evil, with the degree of injury the only variable. Anyone who will attempt to define evil as depending on injury done or on the "intent" of the doer will find the argument gets awfully murky in a hurry.

Many, many people who saw *Searching for God in America*'s eight interviews judged Colson and Nasr to be the most provocative. Not surprisingly, they were the least ambiguous about the nature of man, or why evil appears to be triumphing:

COLSON: And like it or not, we are sinful. [The] greatest myth of the twentieth century is that man is good and getting better. Hegel was wrong when he said all we have to do is educate ourselves out of sin. The fact of the matter is that we have the most educated century in human history and also the bloodiest. We aren't good. We are sinners in need of the grace of God.

NASR: The fact is that religion has been marginalized in human society; it's for Sunday morning, but the laws on Wall Street have nothing to do with Christ. The few moral laws that remain from the founders of the American Revolution have been challenged during the last decade, and that's why there's such turmoil over the question of abortion and so forth, which is tearing American society apart. Europe—which is even more secularized than America—does not want to be challenged by any other world-view, even one that would be viable and at the same time not secular.

Combine these two insights, and the conclusion is: Man is evil and chooses not to recognize and deal with that condition. The church, which might be in a position to help, is treating the wounded and not fighting the war. To fight the war requires an ability to speak the truth and support that truth with cool reason and persuasive argument. That ability is the responsibility of pastors but is especially the responsibility of Sunday school teachers educating the young.

So once the church has retained its membership, its membership must be willing to do two things consistently: praise God and name evil. That's really all that is required of believers.

Catherine Stimson had listened intently to the panel's three pre-sentations. Each of us on the panel had been asked to address the state of the culture in the United States, and Neal Kozodoy, the editor of *Commentary* magazine, Terry Eastland, a prolific author and writer, and I had all agreed: American society had descended into a fetid swamp of tasteless and often sordid excess. I had delivered my grim recounting of statistics that cannot be blunted by even the cheeriest individual. The slide into moral chaos was rapid and thorough, I argued, and only God could accomplish a change. I was the optimist of the three, with Eastland delivering a measured and thorough critique of the moral collapse and Kozodoy reading an indictment that was by turns painful, funny, and tragic on how high culture had collapsed in the past generation.

Catherine Stimson is an impressive academic who, I think she would agree, can only be characterized as being from the Left. She runs the MacArthur Foundation's Genius Fellowship program, which annually doles out millions to worthies across the continent. As soon as the floor was opened to questions and comments, her hand shot up, and she delivered two comments. First, she noted that the panel was unfortu-nately not "balanced." Three less similar folks could not be gathered if one was looking to geography or educational background, but Ms. Stimson meant that since we all agreed the culture was rotten, we were "unbalanced." (Question: Would a panel that agreed that Stalin was a very bad man lack "balance"?) And then she delivered her judgment.

It occurred to her, she told the audience, that they had just heard from a genre, the "Jeremiad," that had a distinguished pedigree but that ought not to be taken too seriously.

I don't remember much else because I immediately concluded that, although she had meant to critique us, she had labeled us in a complimentary way. Perhaps she had forgotten: Jeremiah was a prophet whose predictions of doom came true.

The three of us had been labeled Jeremiahs because we were diagnosing moral ills and we were predicting evil results from those moral ills. That's actually not a very difficult task. What upsets people, what excited Ms. Stimson, was that we were all engaged in naming evil and doing so in an undiplomatic way.

For at least a generation, Americans in the chattering class have stopped naming evil. Commentators, editors, columnists, and pundits of all sorts have just abandoned the project. It's as though the opinion class became embarrassed at the very thought of being thought squares. Unfortunately for the country, that which is not condemned routinely proliferates. As we close the century, only guns, drunk driving, and cigarettes are thought unambiguously to be evil. A moral consensus exists concerning those things in the opinion class. Everything else . . . well, that's debatable.

This way of thinking is relatively new and very pernicious. We modern folk are quite advanced at draining off the evil in our day. A few centuries ago, basic moral cartography was widely agreed upon. And not just by the religious. Aristotle, in *The Nicomachean Ethics,* stated matter-of-factly that many passions "have names that already imply badness e.g., spite, shamelessness, envy and in the case of actions, adultery, theft, murder; for all of these and such like things imply by their names that they are themselves bad. It is not possible, then, ever to be right with regard to them; one must always be wrong. Nor does goodness or badness with regard to such things depend on committing adultery with the right woman, at the right time, and in the right way, but simply to do any of them is to do wrong."

Mustering Aristotle onto the side of Christian ethics is an unexpected and almost unfair tactic, because most of those bent on denying evil find that their dismissiveness is partly and wholly rooted in unstated assumptions that only the religious are concerned with naming evil and that the religious argue from prejudice and mythology, not reason. But when Aristotle takes the field, the relativists' comfortable air of matching wits with the medievalists vanishes.

Aristotle's flat and conclusive summary is doubly injurious to modern relativists because it is specific. We know what *adultery* is, and it is

as self-evidently bad as *murder*. We cannot mistake Aristotle's meaning. It is evil to cheat on a spouse.

And here's the real fun: Moralists don't even need Aristotle. The
self-evidently bad has always been self-evidently bad and will always be
self-evidently bad, whether or not people in our age choose to name it
as such or not. Moreover, all protestations aside, we all know the self-
evidently bad to be self-evidently bad. Recognition of evil is an intuitive and instant process.

A spectacular but by no means a unique proof of both the intuitive
recognition of evil and the elite media's discomfort with the recognition came in the September 1996 issue of *Harper's* magazine. There are
two exhibits in that issue that require a little description to prove my
point. In that single issue there existed a blistering attack on traditional
morality *and* a stunning, indeed horrifying, example of the depths of
individual depravity. What follows is not for the squeamish, even
though I've abbreviated the profanity the magazine reproduced verba-
tim. If you don't care to deal with the reality of the country's moral
state, then skip to the next chapter. The second example is rough. But,
sad to say, it is representative.

The first exhibit was a lengthy piece in that issue by *Harper's* contributing editor Vince Passaro. It was entitled "Dragon Fiction—The
(Very Lucrative) Advent of the Christian Thriller." Note the parenthetical, by which *Harper's* no doubt intended to convey all the reader
really needs to know. What followed this title was a predictable assault
on Christian novels and the people who write and sell them: "bizarre,"
"cheesoid magic realism," "right-wing," "deadening," "blandly uplift-
ing," "heavy medieval streak," "simplistic and sentimental sense of
evil." So wholly predictable was Passaro's ranting that his editors did
not bother to read closely as he drove over the cliff of excess. The very
best excerpt to savor in this wonderful piece of unveiled bigotry was
this:

> Peretti's books, and all these other Christian thrillers, roughly mirror the
> convictions of some significant portion of the 65 percent of Americans
> who say they believe in the devil and the 86 percent who identify them-
> selves as Christians. These convictions, *strange and paranoid though
> they are* . . .

Stop right there. Unless his editors were asleep, in the phrase I've italicized Passaro then brands as "strange and paranoid" the convictions of all Christians, especially those who say they believe in the devil. There's just no other way to read that paragraph.

Passaro's predictable review is not very interesting and would not warrant even a passing scoff but for its juxtaposition with the boxed entry in the very same issue's "Readings" pages. Under "[Evidence]," on page 23, comes "2 Sick 2 Be 4Gotten:" Again, I must warn the delicate: This excerpt is stiff stuff. It contains an assortment of obscenities and vulgarities I find disgusting. But it is illustrative of the depth of the modern culture's disease and the moral incoherence of *Harper's*:

[Evidence]
2 Sick 2 Be 4Gotten

The following notes were written in the high school yearbooks of Kevin Foster, an eighteen-year-old in Fort Myers, Florida, who is charged with the April 30 killing of his school's band director. The entries, obtained by News-Press *Fort Myers reporters Jim Greenhill and Bob Norman, are part of the evidence compiled in the police investigation of Foster and three of his classmates at Riverdale High School who are also charged with the murder.*

This school year sucked, but it was fun writing satanic s— on your math book. Don't kill yourself during the summer.

Have a totally b——— summer. Keep smoking the crack and keep mutilating small defenseless animals.

You're a homicidal maniac but I like that.

You prejudiced b———. You're a little demented, psychotic, suicidal, maniac bum. But that's why we've been friends all these years. See you over the summer.

You are one sick b——— but you're cool. Castrate a cow for me. Have a happy summer. Don't disembowel your dad.

I hope you have a really cool summer. Try not to mutilate any cats or molest any dogs. Try to grow up this summer. Please don't kill anyone, because I hear it's pretty bad in prison. You don't want to be somebody's girlfriend. Seriously, I hope you make something out of your life.

When you grow up you're going to be a homeless, pointless bum. But who cares.

Now we need to focus on some points.

First, *Harper's* Passaro has flung thousands of intemperate and bigoted words against the form of the Christian novel and the people who read Christian novels.

Second, Passaro has ultimately denounced the convictions of Christians generally and those who believe in the devil specifically as "strange and paranoid."

Third, in the same issue the editors hold up as "evidence"—their term, not mine—a shocking display of evil under the banner "2 SICK 2 BE 4GOTTEN."

Harper's can only be judged to be deep in the grip of cognitive dissonance—the psychological condition of holding firm to two impossible-to-reconcile beliefs. I have saved Passaro's concluding remarks until now:

What we learn from this mere blossoming of "Christian fiction" is that American Christianity has entered a paranoid and deeply disgruntled stage, one not helped by the transparently dishonest pieties of politicians who cater to the nation's most superficial moral conviction while ignoring at every turn the deeper requirements those convictions carry. As always, though, we get the leadership that we wish for and deserve: one that doesn't ask much and as we live in a country that wants its narratives sentimental and its religion easy. It has long been so.

So contributing editor Passaro capped off his ramblings with a return to the accusation of paranoia (and with a quite unintentional, I'm sure, kick in the knees for Bill Clinton if "leadership" is understood as including the presidency). What is remarkable about this piece, its juxtaposition with the "Readings" selection, and, indeed, the whole magazine, is the total collapse of moral certainty in the project.

Look. *Harper's* tells us what is, in its contributing editor's view, bad— Christian novels and Christians generally. And the magazine hints at what is shocking and probably bad—a deranged, possibly satanic, and certainly homicidal teenager in Florida. But it cannot tell us what is good. Oh, Passaro likes a few modern novelists. But this is the key problem with our cultural leadership: *Harper's* stands for nothing except a certain tone. It is the tone of tortured ambivalence, partner to that anguished vision that can take in all sides of an argument. It is the ennui of the hypocrite that drenches the entire enterprise.

Lewis Lapham is the magazine's editor, and he contributes a column each month. In this same issue he wrote —beautifully, I should add, for I'm not disputing his or Passaro's writing talent—about self-promotion and flattery. The piece is astonishing if only in the number of targets it assaults, including (and in order of appearance in the essay): Bill Boymers, Barbara Walters, Henry Kissinger, Ben Bradlee, Bill Clinton, Liz Smith, Bob Woodward, Larry King, Alfonse D'Amato, Cindy Crawford, Lee Iacocca, Alexander Haig, Peter Jennings, Sam Donaldson, George Bush, Richard Nixon, Colin Powell, Diane Sawyer, Oprah Winfrey, and Wayne Gretzky. Lapham dispatches them all to the land of "The American Courtier."

It is impossible to miss the dismissive snobbery of Lapham's tone. But just as it's impossible to miss, it's also too much to demand that a reader forget that tone on pages 10, 11, and 12 when he or she comes to page 69 and finds there an advertisement for the Ford Hall Forum to be held at Boston's Faneuil Hall on October 3, 1996. The grabber headline is: WHAT CITIZENS NEED TO KNOW FOR THE FUTURE OF DEMOCRACY. The text is unintentionally hilarious when read immediately after Lapham's assault on self-promotion:

> The Ford Hall Forum and *Harper's Magazine* will present a public program entitled, *Lessons from the Past: What Citizens Need to Know for the Future of Democracy.* Panelists will include John Kenneth Galbraith and Arthur Schlesinger Jr. *Harper's* editor Lewis H. Lapham will chair the discussion.

The Ford Hall Forum is the oldest public lecture series in the nation, and throughout its history the Forum has often stood on the cutting edge of issues vital to America and the world. Past speakers have included Eleanor Roosevelt, Barbara Tuchman, Elie Wiesel, Malcolm X, and Vice President Albert Gore, Jr.

I actually felt sorry for Lapham, who could not have known this ad would run within a few dozen pages of his blistering critique of preening. But his unkindness toward so many received its reward, and again his magazine is exposed chiefly as being incoherent.

It is this incoherence about good and bad that paralyzes our times and our ability to confront evil. That which cannot even be named can hardly be combated. "The devil being everywhere, it's in his interest to be denied," the Islamic scholar Dr. Nasr told me. Perhaps it takes an exiled Muslim to see clearly through the mess that is "Christian" America. The country's squalor is similar to Edgar Allan Poe's "Purloined Letter" — hidden only by its very obvious location.

Harper's is, along with a handful of other magazines, one of the country's leading institutions of elite opinion, like its cousins—the *New York Times,* Harvard University, the Council on Foreign Relations, etc. The editors of *Harper's* comprise a portion of the American elite that collectively define problems and pose solutions. There is no uniformity of opinion within this elite, but it does have dominant attitudes. This "overclass" is greatly suspicious of traditional norms of good and evil. That suspicion is at least in part a fear of anti-intellectual bent to some religious belief. But it is more. It is also a fear of status loss. Large segments of the overclass would rather be in opposition to history's greatest thinkers than to oppose their colleagues' unspoken but deeply held assumptions concerning status.

And because status has been defined as at least partially a function of "tolerance" of all behaviors and attitudes, the overclass has lost its willingness and even perhaps its ability to name evil except in the most obvious of situations.

This collapse of spine among the overclass does not explain the loss of courage among educated believers. I have to wonder how many thousands of "Christians" read Passaro's vicious assault on their fellow believers and did nothing. How many millions on a daily basis see the basest sort of evil and just pass by, either out of laziness or a fear of being thought a fanatic?

This is primarily a problem with Christians whose professional lives and secular obligations oblige them to move in higher circles of business or in social circles that include many non-Christians. It's easier to be adamant about morals in a smaller universe. And the costs of moral explicitness are higher in these settings. But so, too, are the stakes. In fact, the reason we need to name evil more often and with more vigor is because the world needs warning. If tradition is true, if classical theology is not hokum, then sin is not just evil, it has evil consequences that will last an eternity.

T he greatest theological difference between American Christians living at the end of the nineteenth century and those living now seems to be in the way both groups think, or thought, of hell. No doubt there are millions of examples from both groups who would agree on the concept and its implications; but having read widely in the offerings of a century ago, and living among and talking with the believers of today, I am certain that hell, as a persuasive idea, is on its back.

Few things depend upon opinion for their existence. Whether or not people believe Beijing exists, for example, will not in any way affect Beijing's existence. It will still be there even if every American concludes tomorrow that Beijing does not exist and never has.

In the second half of this century, however, hell went from being a place to being a idea, and a not very persuasive idea at that. "I'm not into hell," is one common statement. "I have trouble with a God who would allow hell," goes another.

When hell became an idea instead of a place, it lost much of its hold on folks. Ideas can and have propelled people to act or to refrain from acting. But not ideas that were once believed to be true. Ideas that were once believed to be true but have fallen into the category of myth or fable lose their power to motivate.

This is unfortunate in two respects. First, even if hell is a myth, it served a wonderful purpose of keeping evil in check by means of fear. The objection arrives that it also tormented the overly fearful. Perhaps. But if there was that cost, most utilitarians would have to guess that the benefits in deterrence were greater than the cost in forgone innocent pleasure.

The second unfortunate result is far more serious. It is attributed to Henry Kissinger that he would underscore an argument or assertion with the exclamation that "it has the additional benefit of being true." What if the idea of hell has the additional benefit of being true?

Honestly, ponder that idea for a moment. Put the book down and think: What if hell exists?

Having picked up the book again, I'm guessing that you have consoled yourself with either the thought that it couldn't possibly be true, or if true, that it's not all that bad a place.

Christians, of course, are obliged to believe in hell because Jesus spoke of it. And if Jesus spoke of it, and you believe in the divinity of Jesus, well then, you get the picture.

Here's what He said:

> Then he will say to those at his left hand, "You that are accursed, depart from me into the eternal fire prepared for the devil and his angels; for I was hungry and you gave me no food, I was thirsty and you gave me nothing to drink, I was a stranger and you did not welcome me, naked and you did not give me clothing, sick and in prison and you did not visit me!" Then they also will answer, "Lord, when was it that we saw you hungry or thirsty or a stranger or naked or sick or in prison, and did not take care of you?" Then he will answer them, "Truly, I tell you, just as you did not do it to one of the least of these, you did not do it to me." And these will go away into eternal punishment, but the righteous into eternal life. (Matthew 25:41–46 NRSV)

There's just no way around this. Unless Jesus is in the habit of not meaning what He says, then He means for us to understand that there is hell, a place of "eternal fire," a place of "eternal punishment."

For centuries Christians took Christ at His word, and they understood that hell presented unimaginable horrors. Even though the Reformation occurred and can in one sense be understood as an epochal battle on which method of avoiding hell worked and which did not, both sides agreed that the hell that Jesus described was real.

There arose, in fact, an enormous literature of hell, including first-person accounts of visions of the place, fictional portraits, and theological writings. Some examples are particularly vivid:

> When a damned soul shall shed tears enough to fill all the rivers of the world, even it should shed but one a century, he will be no nearer

deliverance after so many millions of years; he will only have begun to suffer.

—Dominique Bouhours

A vast, unbottom'd, boundless pit,
  Fill'd fou o'lowin' brunstone
Wha's ragin' flame an' scorchin' heat,
  Wad melt the hardest whunstone.

—Robert Burns

I see a brimstone sea of boiling fire
And fiends, with knotted whips of flaming wire,
Torturing poor souls, that gnash their teeth in vain,
And gnaw their flame-tormented tongues for pain.

—Frances Quarles

Saint Theresa of Avila was a Spanish mystic who recorded this version of hell:

The entrance, I thought, resembled a very long, narrow passage, like a furnace, very low, dark, and closely confined; the ground seemed to be full of water which looked like filthy, evil-smelling mud, and in it were many wicked-looking reptiles. At the end there was a hollow place scooped out of a wall, like a cupboard, and it was here that I found myself in close confinement. . . . I felt a fire within my soul the nature of which I am utterly incapable of describing. My bodily sufferings were so intolerable that, though in my life I have endured the severest sufferings of this kind—the worst it is possible to endure, the doctors say, such as the shrinking of the nerves during my paralysis and many and divers more, some of them, as I have said, caused by the devil—none of them is of the smallest account by comparison with what I felt then, to say nothing of the knowledge that they would be endless and never-ceasing. And even these are nothing by comparison with the agony of my soul, an oppression, a suffocation and an affliction so deeply felt, and accompanied by such hopeless and distressing misery, that I cannot too forcibly describe it. . . . In that pestilential spot, where I was quite powerless to hope for comfort, it was impossible to sit or lie, for there was no room to do so. I had been put in this place, which looked like a hole in the wall, and it completely stifled me. There was no light and everything was in the blackest darkness. I do not understand how this can be, but, although there was no light, it was possible to see everything the sight of which can cause affliction. At that time it was not the Lord's will that I should see more of Hell itself, but I have since seen another vision of frightful things, which are the punishment of certain vices. . . . I was terrified by all this, and, here, fear seems to be depriving my body of its natural warmth. I never recall any time when I have been suffering trials or pains and when everything that we can suffer on earth has seemed to me of the slightest importance by comparison with this; so, in a way, I think we complain without reason. I repeat, then, that this vision was one of the most signal favours which the Lord has bestowed upon me: it has been of the greatest benefit to me, both in taking from me all fear of the tribulations and disappointments of this life and also in strengthening me to suffer them and to give thanks to the Lord.

Contrast these very descriptive and indeed terrifying accounts of hell with three of modernity's offerings:

In Hell there is no hope and consequently no duty, no work, nothing to be gained by praying, nothing to be lost doing what you like. Hell, in short, being a place where you have nothing to do but amuse yourself, is the paradise of the worthless.

—George Bernard Shaw

Hell is other people.
—Jean Paul Sartre

> *What is Hell? Hell is oneself,*
> *Hell is alone, the other figures in it*
>   *merely projections. There is nothing to*
>   *escape from and nothing to escape to.*
> *One is always alone.*

—T. S. Eliot

If modernists had set out with the intention of destroying the reality of hell, they could not have done so more effectively than with the above examples.

The greatest theologians built a wall around the idea of hell. They wished to protect it—to encourage its contemplation. Augustine said, "Anyone who thinks that such damnation is excessive or unjust clearly does not know how to measure how great was the wickedness in sinning where it was so easy not to sin." And Aquinas added, "That the saints may enjoy their beatitude and the grace of God more abundantly, they are permitted to see the punishment of the damned in Hell." This last statement by Aquinas is particularly harsh to modern ears, where the idea of joy rooted in the contemplation of *just* suffering is alien, because very little suffering is thought just.

The literature about hell and the scholarship concerning it is vast, if generally unknown. When I sent my research assistant off to retrieve some of the basics, he produced in short order forty-five selections, as chilling an array of descriptions of that place as has ever been collected in a single binder. It is stunning, this amnesia in the West and especially the United States, as to the stakes involved. We are amnesiacs because our intellectual elite has gradually and carelessly allowed an indifference to the possibilities to take root.

This is not the fault of the disbelievers. Were it only the disbelievers who had attempted the overthrow of hell while also overthrowing heaven and God, who could complain? They do not believe, and they believe belief to be injurious. In an odd sort of way, the genuine atheists and hedonists can be understood even as they are pitied.

But believers have overthrown hell in our era. That is the scandal. Because many, many people "have a problem with hell" and judge it medieval, backwards, so "retro" that the church has thrown it overboard.

If hell were alive, if even only a small percentage of Christians found it a motivating force, would the world improve? Of course. Would some additional individuals be obliged to search with greater fervor for the searching God? Of course. Would many of the modern diseases of apathy, lethargy, and envy disappear? Of course.

But it is unlikely to happen, this resurrection of hell. Those who might raise the serious theological question of whether hell ought to be understood as it was understood for close to two thousand years will find in their paths an incredible outpouring of calumny. Defined in its nonthreatening form, hell has been drained of its fury and, truth be told, of its fear-inspiring qualities. Revive it, and you revive fear of consequences. Revive fear of consequences, and folks will want stern and straight talk about the actions that lead to the fearful consequences. Before you know it, traditional morality would resurface and with it, the end of ambiguity about good and bad. The road back to hell would be paved with denunciations of social science and pop psychology as well as of most modern entertainments.

It's hard to imagine such a result. Harder, really, than imagining hell. Which is the irony.

But even if the return of hell did not accomplish much in the way of a resurgent moral sense, still it would deserve a few kind words. Why? Because God intends mankind to believe in hell. Christ intends it. Millions of believers are abandoning a duty to warn the world, and especially their fellow Christians, of the perils of sin. If hell exists and if embarrassed silence in any way abets the eternal damnation of souls, how will the genuine cost of that embarrassment be reckoned? Ask yourself this impossible question (we all fail this test): If bold witness assists in the salvation of one person and yet costs the witness everything, is it not still the most magnificent bargain possible? Ecclesiastes teaches us that the witness has nothing to lose anyway, since "all is . . . a chasing after wind." But the soul in peril that is pulled back is infinitely— literally—blessed.

23

Preachers Don't Curse

Bold witness by confident Christians will regenerate the culture even as it brings souls into eternal union with Christ. Evidence of the culture-renewing potential of faith is all around us. Here's a bulletin for you: Preachers—and rabbis and Buddhist monks and Mormon apostles and Sufi scholars—don't curse. They don't use profanity of either the lesser or the greater variety.

Here's another stunner: People in the presence of all the above, overtly religious people don't curse. In hours and hours of taping and setup that went into *Searching for God in America,* I don't recall a single instance when any of the technical crew or the associated workers and helpers used even coarse language.

If you have the book *Searching for God in America,* go in search of profanity in the interviews. It's not there in the transcripts, and I don't recall it's finding its way into the anthology either.

Contrast this rectitude in speech with what you will hear around you today. Here is one area where television has not led the pack on the rush to the bottom. Television remains rather civilized, almost prudish, on matters of language. But between people, and especially in books and magazines, all standards have been exiled. I am no longer shocked to find the coarsest language in, say, the *New Republic.* The *New Republic* will be only quoting, but it will do so without sparing the reader a collision with profanity—a new policy, I think, but even if an old one, the occasions when the use of profanity in this venerable magazine arise are growing more frequent.

But coarseness does not happen around preachers, an interruption of standard practice that merits some attention. Obviously, those who would otherwise use profanity do not do so for one of two reasons: Either they are solicitous of the preacher, or they are ashamed of their own language. The idea of that solicitousness at work is not easy to defend. It is, for instance, hard to imagine people worrying about the tender ears of Chuck Colson, who not only spent most of his pre-conversion life in the salty warrens of politics but who spends a great deal of his post-conversion life in the company of the toughest men in the toughest places in the world—prisons.

No, I think most people who swear except in the presence of preachers (and the elderly, kids, or their own parents), refrain from doing so out of shame. Now we have to ask, why the shame? The answer is crucial to understanding the power of bold witness and to the project of defending belief.

The too-easy answer, offered by the resolutely nonreligious, is that it is shameful to use the language of the uneducated. But of course a lot of very educated people, whose intelligence cannot be doubted or unknown, leave off swearing in some precincts. Why do very sharp folks who curse like sailors not do so in the presence of the cloth?

A more elaborate, psychology-based explanation argues that well-developed techniques of socialization trigger the suppression of behaviors like swearing, which would engender a negative reaction. But this can serve at best as only a partial explanation unless those who don't swear around religious figures also never swear around strangers.

No, the real reason is that shame silences the foul-mouthed in the presence of folks who, by virtue of their calling, are generally going to be upright and righteous.

Shame at the use of profanity is an appropriate response, because it is an evil habit—an unthinking retreat from civility to brutishness. It is doubly shameful when practiced by individuals quite capable of using non-profane speech to underscore emphasis.

But it is at its worst when the cursing involves God's name or the simple but highly offensive use of the name Jesus Christ to express anger, frustration, shock, or dismay.

A quaint point, our cognoscenti will think to themselves. But given their own philosophy—wherein tolerance is everything, wherein tolerance remains the *only* value—their use of sacred names for profane purposes is not only simply evil, it is bottomed by hypocrisy as well. Nothing so offends the genuinely religious as the use of religious imaging in profane projects. If the National Endowment for the Arts continues its crumbling, it will be because of its coarseness but especially because some of that coarseness has also been blasphemous, and there are enough bold believers around to still cry "Foul!" effectively.

If, however, the *real* project of the tolerance police is the draining off of the vestiges of morality that hold back human behavior from evil and that incapacitates moral judgment, then the routine trampling of speech beneath obscenity and especially the debasement of sacred names serves that end quite nicely. It is difficult to maintain serious respect for a name that is routinely trashed.

Nowhere is the collapse of restraint in speech more pronounced than in the offices of "journalism." I've roamed a dozen studios and newsrooms and have experienced firsthand the coarseness of speech and humor there. The defense of this level of incivility is that it is the tradition of the profession to be profane, to be hard-livers and hard-drinkers.

Whatever the reason, it is unfortunate that those charged with reporting the news and creating visual and auditory entertainment have lost their sense of shame in such matters. The "culture" so many fret about cannot possibly be healed if even its educated guardians employ the language of the coarsest subset of the population and if the same group sees no harm in the routine profanity of the sacred.

But nothing is more quickly or easily suppressed than profanity of this sort. If a believer—backed by his or her own example—merely mentions the discomfort caused by the resort to profane language, the offending speaker is more likely than not to cease the practice. The retreats in the face of even gentle reproaches on this subject that I have witnessed have been complete. The specific, direct request not to use Christ's name as a profanity maneuvers the offending party into a choice between discussing theology or choosing silence. The latter is powerfully attractive to the insecure. If you have any doubts, bring a pastor along on a lunch outing with your most profane colleague. Later on ask why it was your colleague with the proclivity for profanity suddenly rediscovered civility.

And there's the hidden strength of belief that embarrassed believers must grasp. Most men and women know—they just intuitively know—that dedicated people of faith are not to be trifled with. There are exceptions, but their numbers are astonishingly few. Boldness in declaring faith is its own best protection. It can silence profanity. And it can change lives. But only if it is sincerely held and boldly proclaimed. For too many years the moral project was orphaned, and then it came under the care of friendly but uncommitted leadership. It is the hardest lesson of all for EBs to grasp, but they must not put their hope for the city, state, or country into the hands of purely secular leadership. It's not the politicians who can right the upended or undo the damage. It's not the intellectuals, and it's not the "civic" leaders. But EBs can do it for themselves and for others if they find their courage and if their leaders lead. It is impossible to restore an absolute morality unless the architects are themselves committed to the same restoration. That is, unless the leaders genuinely believe in the morality themselves.

24

ALLIES, BUT NOT BELIEVERS

I f the name of Gertrude Himmelfarb is new to you, then you need to know that she is among the country's first rank of historians.

If the name Francis Fukuyama is new to you, then you need to know that he is among the country's first rank of political philosophers.

Both are authors, and their unwieldy names are attached to unwieldy books, but books of great importance.

Himmelfarb's 1994 book, *The De-Moralization of Society,* charts the destruction of absolutes in our day and defends the much-sneered-at Victorians from various idiot libels. "So long as morality was couched in the language of 'virtue,'" she wrote, "it had a firm, resolute character." Once Nietzsche and the social scientists had thrown "virtue" overboard in favor of "values," she concludes, all hell broke loose as "'values' brought with it the assumptions that all moral ideas are subjective and relative, that they are mere customs and conventions, that they have a purely instrumental, utilitarian purpose, and that they are peculiar to specific individuals and societies."

Fukuyama's 1992 book, *The End of History and the Last Man,* is nobody's idea of a beach-read. It is so dense, in fact, that its bestseller status is itself astonishing.

But for the diligent reader willing to work through it, there is a pay-off in Fukuyama's prose—an understanding of the modern predicament.

"Morality," concluded Fukuyama, "involves a distinction between better and worse, good and bad, which seems to violate the democratic principle of tolerance. It is for that reason that the last man becomes concerned above all for his own personal health and safety, because it is uncontroversial. In America today, we feel entitled to criticize another person's smoking habits, but not his or her religious beliefs or moral behavior. For Americans, the health of their bodies—what they eat and drink, the exercise they get, the shape they are in—has become a far greater obsession than the moral questions that tormented their forebears."

Himmelfarb and Fukuyama were both the recipients of many glowing book reviews and the subject of many seminar discussions. Their status as observers of the collapse of morality is unchallenged. But the apparent impact of their books on the culture is zero. They launched well-aimed, well-argued missiles at the decay in the country, but the missiles turned out to be duds. They sold a few books. A few heads turned. Big deal.

Then there's William Bennett—a champion of all virtuecrats, whom I called a "general" earlier in this book. *The Book of Virtues* soared to the top of all bestseller lists and stayed there. The book became a cartoon series for PBS, and Bennett became the closest thing to a national chaplain—heavily secularized—that the country has ever had. Again, though, the big question is whether or not the virtue bubble he inspired brought about change in the culture at large.

James Q. Wilson, another social scientist and moralist, launched his book *The Moral Sense* in 1993. Its opening line reads: "Virtue has acquired a bad name." His purpose was "to help people recover the confidence with which they once spoke about virtue and morality." Wilson concludes the work with the rather remarkable statement that "a good character, however defined, is not life lived according to a rule (there rarely is a rule by which good qualities ought to be combined or hard choices resolved), it is a life lived in balance." Conventional Christian morality would argue that there's hardly any "balance" at all in "obedience," but Wilson's conclusions are separate from his impact. As with the preceding entries into the intellectual fray, Wilson's efforts do not appear to have brought forth fruit.

One book did make something of a dent: Stephen Carter's *The Culture of Disbelief.* Carter, a professor of law at Yale Law School, wrote an entire book addressing the question, "How did we reach this disturbing pass, when our culture teaches that religion is not to be taken seriously, even by those who profess to believe in it?" Carter's legal analysis is not what mattered in his book. Rather, his title named a condition, and the title stuck. Many who never read the book can recall that it refers to an almost prosecutorial zeal on the part of intellectual elites to strip serious conversation of God from the public conversation. That's no small achievement to name a disease. But crucially, it's also no cure.

In the course of 1996 a new entrant in the lists arrived: Robert Bork's *Slouching towards Gomorrah*. Another provocative title. Another wonderful read. The question is: Was this another blank fired at a moving target?

Judge Bork's words are quite bold: "We are well along the road to the moral chaos that is the end of radical individualism and the tyranny that is the goal of radical egalitarianism." "Modern liberalism," Bork concluded, "has corrupted our culture across the board." Bork goes on to predict the arrival of "a new Dark Ages."

For a brief moment Bork's book became significantly different from whose that went before it:

> Perhaps the most promising development in our time is the rise of an energetic, optimistic, and politically sophisticated religious conservatism. . . . The Christian Coalition, the Catholic Campaign for America, and the resurgence of interest among the young in Orthodox Judaism are all signs that religion is gaining strength, and religious precepts will eventually influence political action.

Having come closer than anyone to announcing the obvious, however, Bork then retreats: "Religion is, of course, not the only source of morality," he is quick to add, as though he had suddenly become afraid of his own conclusion. "In a word," he summarizes, "everything ultimately depends on the temper of the American people."

Well, then, all is lost. The "temper of the American people" is not a bulwark on which I place much hope. While Bork veered toward religious renewal as the key to the future, he flinched when it came time to sum up.

Why is that? Why did Professor Carter, whose book was launched so well with an explicit expression of his faith, then abandon the effort to argue for a transcendent "truth" above all other truths? Professor Carter, in fact, uses the parenthetical as a shield against the charge of intolerance. One example:

The argument runs, only Christians —people who profess a faith in Jesus Christ as Son of God and Savior—can achieve eternal life. Many Christians do in fact believe this, citing, for example, John 14:6 as authority. (My own view is that exclusivity of this kind betrays a lack of faith in God's charity, but everyone is entitled to choose a religious belief.)

Professor Carter is a very likable man, a wonderful guest on my show, and I do not doubt the fervor of his own belief. But where Carter, and indeed all of these "public intellectuals," have failed the public is in writing books that condemn a moral relativism they themselves are embracing, though in a less obvious way. That's the problem, and it is a large one. Himmelfarb, Fukuyama, Bennett, Carter, and Bork tried to have it both ways. They wanted to scorn moral relativism without explicitly declaring the alternative.

Not one of these authors argues for the superior truth of either the gospel or the Talmud or the Koran. Certainly there are nods toward the utility of these writings. And there is an appreciation for the constructive role to be played by those who do believe in the absolute authenticity of Yahweh or Jesus as the Christ. But there is no apologetic content to these writings. And as they are mute on the ultimate question, they are ineffective. In fact, they may actually be harmful. Because if Gertrude Himmelfarb, Francis Fukuyama, William Bennett, James Q. Wilson, Stephen Carter, and Robert Bork cannot muster from among themselves a defense of the proposition that God exists and He commands obedience to His law, well then, how true can such a proposition be? If these half-dozen virtue "superstars" will not make the case that C. S. Lewis made, then why not conclude there is no case to be made? Was C. S. Lewis that much more courageous then these folks?

It is possible to argue, especially with regard to Professor Carter, that I am being unfair by criticizing authors for not writing books different from those they were writing. Perhaps it is unfair. But each in his or her own way set out to diagnose the disease that is killing the culture—by that I mean the destruction of our moral sense and thus our ability to sense God even as He pursues us—and each ended up cataloging symptoms and/or explaining the root causes. The cures that were offered were either (a) incomplete in that these various intellectuals left out faith, or (b) complete but disappointing because the authors do not believe in faith's power or its truth.

I suspect the latter. I do so out of respect for the intellectual courage of the bunch who have not hesitated to wade into various fights with both arms swinging. Combatants all, it would be profoundly dispiriting to think that they did not press the case for God because they were embarrassed to do so.

So there must not in their eyes be such a case to make. They may object that personal religion is, for them, a private matter—no hearts-on-sleeves for them. But that would be inconsistent with their "public" status.

No, I suspect they are ready to cheer on God's troops—to review, especially the excerpt from Bork—but not to cheer on God. In the troops they can believe. But in God, well . . .

And there is the rub. In recent years the party of the right placed its bet on reason alone and not on reason buttressed by and enhanced with divine revelation. The leadership threw in with the idea that men could have wisdom and could choose rightly when it came to rulers and laws. Believers have been welcomed along as foot soldiers and useful troops but not because what they believe to be true is true. And, as a result, the disease has grown worse. The alliance between reason and revelation was allowed to decay, and reason cannot sustain a nation.

Look here: The greatest American, Abraham Lincoln, spoke to this issue more than 130 years ago. If you carry away from this book nothing else, try and keep something from Lincoln's Proclamation Appointing a National Fast Day on March 30, 1863:

> Whereas, the Senate of the United States, devoutly recognizing the Supreme Authority and just Government of Almighty God, in all the affairs of men and of nations, has, by a resolution, requested the President to designate and set apart a day for National prayer and humiliation.
>
> And whereas it is the duty of nations as well as of men, to own their dependence upon the overruling power of God, to confess their sins and transgressions, in humble sorrow, yet with assured hope that genuine repentance will lead to mercy and pardon; and to recognize the sublime

truth, announced in the Holy Scriptures and proven by all history, that those nations only are blessed whose God is the Lord.

And, insomuch as we know that, by His divine law, nations like individuals are subjected to punishments and chastisements in this world, may we not justly fear that the awful calamity of civil war, which now desolates the land, may be but a punishment, inflicted upon us, for our presumptuous sins, to the needful end of our national reformation as a whole People? We have been the recipients of choicest bounties of Heaven. We have been preserved, these many years, in peace and prosperity. We have grown in numbers, wealth and power, as no other nation has ever grown. But we have forgotten God. We have forgotten the gracious hand which preserved us in peace, and multiplied and enriched and strengthened us; and we have vainly imagined, in the deceitfulness of our hearts, that all these blessings were produced by some superior wisdom and virtue of our own. Intoxicated with unbroken success, we have become too self-sufficient to feel the necessity of redeeming and preserving grace, too proud to pray to the God that made us!

It behooves us then, to humble ourselves before the offended Power, to confess our national sins, and to pray for clemency and forgiveness.

Now, therefore . . . I do, by this my proclamation, designate and set apart Thursday, the 30th day of April, 1863, as a day of national humiliation, fasting and prayer. And I do hereby request all the People to abstain, on that day, from their ordinary secular pursuits, and to unite, at their several places of public worship and their respective homes, in keeping the day holy to the Lord, and devoted to the humble discharge of the religious duties proper to that solemn occasion.

Let us then rest humbly in the hope authorized by the Divine teachings, that the united cry of the Nation will be heard on high, and answered with blessings, no less than the pardon of our national sins, and the restoration of our now divided and suffering Country, to its former happy condition of unity and peace.

Anyone who knows even a bit about Lincoln will know that this proclamation is not like our modern presidential proclamations. Why? Because Lincoln himself wrote it, and he intended it to be read and studied. And in it he stressed the root problem of a country engaged in a bloody and devastating Civil War: "We have grown in numbers, wealth and power, as no other nation has ever grown. But we have for-gotten God."

In recent years a religious awakening has begun that can profoundly affect the culture, but not if those who attempt to steer that powerful force do not themselves authentically believe. Indeed, even if the same proclamation that was issued by Lincoln were issued by a president today, the outrage that would overwhelm such a president would be unprecedented. So we cannot expect another Lincoln to arrive and diagnose the problems and pursue their solutions with purpose and clarity. The leadership will not come from Washington, D.C.

On a personal level, the most astonishing lesson for me to arrive from the year-long process of putting together *Searching for God in America* was the recognition of the utter impotence of modern politics and political theory in the face of virulent evil. It's been a rout for twenty-five years. Even as Western political theory appeared to tri-umph with the collapse of communism, the evil of the East had set up shop in the West under a widely different name and approach. Political totalitarianism collapsed even as cultural totalitarians bent on the destruction of faith were cresting. I have a friend, Bob Fry, who likes to say that the Berlin Wall collapsed with the assistance of the devil because the devil was doing better on our side. You have to wonder.

It did not work, the misplaced faith in politics. Perhaps it's time to try faith in faith, and faith alone. Chuck Colson hinted as much to me when he said, "What we're watching in Washington right now is a debate between right-wing utopians and left-wing utopians. The left-wingers thought we could produce the perfect state and the Great Society. The right-wingers say we can create incentives to responsible behavior by re-engineering. They're all social engineers. They're all utopians."

At a minimum, those who lead need fearlessly to reconnect reason and revelation, as did Lincoln. It would be a good question, I think, to pose to those who would lead in politics if they agree that Lincoln's proclamation of 1863 has any relevance today. The answers, I think, would disappoint.

J ohn Churchill, the first Duke of Marlborough, is a figure generally unknown in the modern era. For the better part of twenty years, however, he dominated England and Europe. Clearly, he changed history's course.

In a decade of war against the armies of Louis XIV, he won many significant victories. The names of Ramillies, Oudenaarde, and Malplaquet are today hardly pronounceable in the United States—certainly I can't get them right—much less understood, but they are milestones in Europe's and the world's history. Marlborough's greatest victory, however, was at Blenheim. To reach that German town, the Duke had conducted a speedy and wholly unexpected march of hundreds of miles across the center of Europe. The combat there on August 13, 1704, was terrible and full of slaughter. "Blenheim is immortal as a battle," wrote Winston Churchill—the Duke's descendant—230 years later, "not only because of the extraordinary severity of the fighting of all the troops on the field all day long, and the overwhelming character of the victory, but because it changed the political axis of the world."

Writing his biography of Marlborough just a few years before World War II enveloped Europe, Churchill could, without a hint of irony, begin the chapter devoted to Blenheim in this fashion:

Marlborough had spent some of the night in prayer. He received the sacrament from Dr. Hare. "The religion he had learned as a boy" fortified his resolution and sealed his calm.

Three observations sprang from these lines:

First, we ought not to be surprised by Churchill's approach to the opening of this critical portion of narrative. Faith occupied a crucial space in the private and public lives and debates of Marlborough's era.

Just a couple of years prior to Blenheim, the Duke had been deeply enmeshed in a pitched *political* battle that deeply divided England. The Occasional Conformity Bill of 1702 sought to penalize non-Anglican Protestants who nevertheless wished to hold public office and thus took Anglican Communion at least occasionally. The bill proposed to fine such "occasional conformists," and it set Whig against Tory and the Queen against many of her ministers. To ears of our day it seems incredibly far-fetched that anyone would be obliged to take Communion at all in order to hold public office, much less a particular kind of Communion. That such debates did indeed matter and not only mattered but mattered greatly underscores the seriousness with which doctrine was contemplated. Because God was real and immediate to those people, they took seriously—even to the point of violence—the gospel.

Second, Marlborough's reliance on God was not feigned. From all we know of his practice (and we know quite a lot—biographers have been plowing this field for centuries), his personal faith was real and deeply held. While our commanders and leaders may still be deeply religious, it is difficult for many to imagine Norman Schwarzkopf, for instance, receiving Communion on the eve of battle. Actually, it is more difficult imagining Schwarzkopf's allowing anyone to know that he had received Communion than it is to imagine that the general had actually engaged in religious ritual on the eve of battle. The Pentagon, aware of the dominant media culture's attitude toward faith, could hardly be indifferent to such an event as Communion-taking on the eve of Desert Storm. If a commander in the modern age were known by the media to be deeply religious, inevitably questions would be raised as to that commander's judgment and competence. The deep thinkers on the networks would be wondering aloud whether such a general's judgment might be compromised by his faith.

Finally, the biographer's treatment of the incident is also telling as to the audience of the early 1930s. Churchill *began* the critical chapter with the moment of faith. The biographer's art allows for many openings of critical moments. Winston Churchill's use of John Churchill's prayer suggests that the former—a sympathetic biographer—understood the religious practice of the latter to be both routine and comforting to the reader of the day.

Marlborough was aimed at an audience that would read of such a faith and note it as *unexceptional* and certainly *uncontroversial*. The biographer was not making a statement that stunned readers. Churchill quickly moved on to the mechanics of battle and the communications between the Duke and his ally, Prince Eugene of Austria.

Such an introductory stroke in a biography today would sound a clunker. In fact, try and find in the biography of any modern public figure whose career is not explicitly tied to faith any nonjudgmental, non-analytical, matter-of-fact reference to religious practice. They may exist. I have not found one. Imagine the paragraph quoted, substituting Schwarzkopf for Marlborough and Desert Storm for Blenheim.

I don't think so. Today's biographers practice an unlicensed psychotherapy with abandon, and none would allow deep and practiced faith to pass without a searching critique. So deep is the modern suspicion of the irrationality of belief that expressions of faith meet not with the nodding recognition accorded the usual and the predictable but with the raised eyebrow that attends sittings of the unusual and the at least slightly scandalous.

Here again is another silent prompt for embarrassment. The messages of the culture do not have to be loud to be heard. And if the embedded narrative—the story line so deeply mixed into daily life—is hostile to faith, we will pick up those signals. As the religious life of political, academic, and artistic elites has gone into hiding, the unmistakable message is that ordinary folks ought to camouflage their beliefs as well. Now ask yourself, did Schwarzkopf attend religious services on the eve of battle? Was there any report to that effect? Did Colin Powell or Secretary of Defense Dick Cheney or President George Bush? Would you have wanted them to? The elite media would not have cottoned to other than a formulaic expression of hope in God's grace, and certainly not to a Christian prayer for victory.

Now that's just the way it is. How we got into such a predicament is a historian's tale. The crucial question, though, is how to recapture the routine respect for God and those who believe in Him so that biographers of our leaders might again begin a chapter devoted to a critical moment with the phrase he "had spent some of the night in prayer."

An eight-year-old watching a movie in the late '90s that attempts to recreate the world of America in 1963—say, Tom Hanks' *That Thing You Do*—will have to make a great leap of faith to believe the world was so antique then. It is probably more difficult for such a child to imagine such a past than it is for him or her to imagine the *Star Trek* future of space travel and other technological marvels.

The culture of 1963 is so alien because it was so calm. The idea of violence happening to innocents traveling on bikes or in cars was unthinkable. At this point it is routine to acknowledge the many ills of that time, foremost among them the dying but still vicious segregation and discrimination practiced toward blacks and all other non-whites. Many women will point as well to the lack of opportunity for them.

But it's impossible to mistake the trend that has marked the years from 1963 forward. Recall the early chapter on trajectory. We return again to that trend. Some good has been accomplished in the last four decades, but much evil has rushed in and over and around every old barricade. "We indeed live in a vulgar age," Supreme Court Justice Antonin Scalia was obliged to remark in a 1992 opinion, but he was far too charitable. We live in a vulgar, diseased, vicious, cruel, indeed an unthinkable age.

And if you want to argue the point, drop off reading now and go to your television. At 5:15 P.M. on October 6, 1996, I did so. After a few commercials, the channel returned to the Music Video Awards. The presenters were rappers Snoop Doggy Dogg and Tupac Shakur. Shakur had been murdered weeks earlier, so this tape was obviously a rebroadcast. The two Death Row Records stars introduced the nominees for the best "Hard Rock Video," nominees that included Alice in Chains, Rage Against the Machine, and Metallica. Metallica's video for "Until It Sleeps" won.

The four-minute sequence of clips from the nominated videos and the winners' acceptance were remarkable only in that the entire performance was unremarkable—wholly predictable in feel, right down to one of Metallica's member's feigned nonchalance conveyed through his eating a banana while accepting the award. The video clips were simply shocking and of no value. The videos were, in a word, evil.

The point is that I randomly picked a tune-in time but was willing to do so, confident that MTV would not disappoint my expectations. It is impossible to get lower than the belly of the hard-rock culture of 1996.

"Our culture is being poisoned," Chuck Colson told me, "with pornography and banality, and people are losing their sense of connectedness." He continued:

> I mean, what makes a society is the belief that we have certain values that we all share and that we inherit these from the past. All of that is crumbling in American life today.
>
> There's moral disintegration going on, and people feel uncertain about their safety. They fear crime. Look at what's happened to the crime rate in America. Violent crime has gone up 560 percent since the sixties. Any day, any of us could have a gun held in our face by a juvenile criminal—a predator 14 to 17 years old. I mean, the numbers in the juvenile crime rate are swelling.

We *know* Colson is correct. As I scribbled the first draft of this chapter, the number of random assaults on motorists in Southern California mushroomed for a few days—a passing fad, yes, but what a passing fad. An unbelievable tragedy occurred— the murder of a young boy by a bullet fired into the van driven by his mother—and wrenched the hearts of all who heard of it. It was simple madness, simple evil.

And it is so routine that I could not locate an account of the tragedy in my morning paper. On the radio, yes, but not in my paper. The attack apparently did not merit comment outside of the metropolitan Los Angeles area.

By the time the manuscript rewrites were done, a friend of mine in politics, a mayor, had led a small town through the agonizing abduction, assault, and murder of a ten-year-old boy, snatched without warning from an afternoon of play with his pals.

In the previous chapter I wondered how routine respect for God could be recaptured, rehabilitated at least to the level that belief was unremarkable, and not the occasion for the kind of scorn one finds in *Harper's*. The second question is how to reintroduce the easy and quick recognition and condemnation of evil. Outrage flares and then rapidly drains away. Every time that sequence recurs, the impact of the outrage is diminished and our patience with perversity expands.

Look. Scripture is fairly specific. Confession and repentance precede forgiveness and renewal—on individual and on national levels. The moral squalor into which we have collectively sunk requires as its remedy, first, a recognition of its existence.

MTV is an evil thing. Only an idiot could not recognize that. How to address that evil may be difficult, and certainly constitutional guarantees dictate that the remedy cannot come from the government. But the devising of remedies cannot begin until we are all agreed on the nature of the beast. The morons among the elites may want to debate particulars, but the vast majority recognize evil and lack only the courage to name it and to announce how far it has spread.

The defense of belief requires those who do hold their faiths to be true to speak true statements about the culture around them. Here is an unpleasant task: To be the scourge, the blue-nose, the Puritan. Except the swamp is so deep that one hardly has to worry about approaching intolerance of the merely tasteless. There's more than enough pure evil to go around without having to attack the merely repulsive elements of the culture.

The idea of playing the Puritan in this culture is not inviting in any way. When a younger pastor of my acquaintance preached a sermon that included a friendly admonition to parents on the need to keep an eye on the computer games their children played, I had some sport with him and named his message "Mike's Jihad Sermon." Of course he was right, and I knew it, and he knew I knew it, but we still chuckled over the notion of a moral crusade.

No one wants to be the Carry Nation of the '90s. Carry Nation launched the mass movement toward Prohibition though she died before its adoption in 1919. Nation combined gospel preaching with hatchet wielding, and perhaps she birthed a whole archetype: The twentieth-century humorless, uncomfortably dressed, religious fanatic out to end everyone's fun. We know from the fact that the most eagerly watched Super Bowl ads come from the beer companies that Nation not only developed a miserable image, she also failed. With a pedigree like that (and its ancestors go way back in the country to the Salem witch trials), no one is going to be the first to rush out and argue for anything approaching serious Puritanism in personal behavior. We'll get the *Book of Virtues* and "character education" past the guardians of taste, but just try abstinence education. While it's exactly what the young men and women of the nation need, the condom lobby has a marathon-length lead.

There is no choice, however, other than a return to rigor in personal conduct and to court the scorn of the anti-Puritans, or to surrender to debasement.

That's what we are talking about: Surrender to widespread, endemic, indeed epidemic, debasement. Sure, there have always been significant corners of debasement in America. But where one had to work to find them even fifty years ago in terms of drugs, sex, or general abandonment of taste, one now has to work hard to avoid debased extremes. It's genuinely doubtful whether they can be avoided.

That's the problem. The retreat of the Puritans has come close to complete surrender in fairly abrupt fashion. The collapse of resistance to debasement occurred between 1965 and 1975, and it was total. Now, however, the Puritans have to demand a rematch.

THE GREAT COMMISSION DID NOT HAVE AN EXPIRATION DATE

T he apparent triumph of evil presents a challenge to Christians. As the culture abandons long-held positions of moral common sense, and as new outrages pile up, it is easy to forget Scripture's repeated admonitions to keep hope alive. Even among those who do so effortlessly, there is a strong pull to withdraw to the islands of sanity—the strong communities of faith—and once there to worship and pray and disengage from the world.

This is the dilemma of the Parallel Culture, which I hinted at many chapters back—the Christian culture that has built for itself a place apart from the moral chaos of our times. In the two years that I pursued my television series and the two connected books (including this one), I came across oasis after oasis of calm, bountiful, and renewing faith. There are communities of Christians who are rallying against the debasement of the culture and the violence of the world. And there is a supporting infrastructure of entertainment, publishing, commerce, and primary, secondary, and higher-education, all devoted to the maintenance of the Parallel Culture. There are indeed tens of millions of wonderful people called by God to live lives obedient to His commands, and they do so. And they have tens of millions of allies around the world.

But even as American Christians have built the Parallel Culture and constructed high walls around it, the ongoing collapse of the broader culture is racing forward. Jack Kevorkian, for example, is quite clearly an evil man blasting past long-held and very generally accepted morals; yet the government is quite incapable of halting conduct that is, to the vast majority of Americans, clearly murder. Partial-birth abortion remains an optional procedure in the face of huge majorities opposed to it (and even larger majorities when educated to the facts of this infanticide by another name). Baseball can't bring itself to suspend its louts, even when the most offensive behavior is filmed and rebroadcast. Worst of all, children routinely impregnate each other and shoot and kill each other.

The collapse of decency is so far advanced, in fact, that the image of monasteries comes to mind again, and not just at colleges devoted to the study of the great books such as Saint John's College. The Parallel Culture of believers and sympathizers (and the just plain scared) are retreating into defensible redoubts and digging deep moats. Of course a remnant will survive—Scripture guarantees it. The temptation to sound retreat is huge.

Against this temptation there are two defenses.

First, the culture can be reclaimed and decency revitalized.

In his 1975 memoir, *The Oak and the Calf,* Aleksandr Solzhenitsyn penned a profound testament to the power of good. In a work published at the apparent height of Soviet power—the invasion of Afghanistan was still five years in the future, and the collapse of the Soviet Empire more than a decade and a half away—Solzhenitsyn included these prophetic words:

> Yes, yes of course—we all know that you cannot poke a stick through the walls of a concrete tower, but here's something to think about: what if those walls are only a painted backdrop?
>
> Looking back, even a fool would be able to predict it today: the Soviet regime could certainly have been breached only by literature. The regime has been reinforced with concrete to such an extent that neither a military coup nor a political organization nor a picket line of strikers can knock it over or run it through. Only the solitary writer would be able to do this. And the Russian younger generation would move on into the breach.
>
> Obvious? Yet no one foresaw it, either in the thirties or in the forties. That's the trouble with the future: it slips away and eludes us.

The power of evil in the West, and specifically in the United States, may be as brittle as the power of the Soviet state was revealed to be in

1989. But even the most atrophied power cannot be shattered if no one takes a hammer to it. People of faith need to swing that hammer but in fairly unpredictable ways. Literature breached the Soviet wall; powerless Jews desiring only to emigrate from the Soviet Union to Israel broke off other pieces. Secretive Lutherans tapped away in places like East Germany as did Catholic shipworkers in Poland and poets in Czechoslovakia. All were encouraged by sympathizers in the West. When the evil in the East began to crumble, it did so with a rapidity that remains breathtaking.

The same could happen here. But only if Christians leave off trying to capture political power and instead target their renewing energy on the culture. I fully believe if the Claremont Consultation (the liberals) and the Christian Coalition (the conservatives) and all other believers in between who were concerned with the culture set themselves the goal of buying majority control of, say, the Times Mirror Corporation with its newspapers—including the *Los Angeles Times*—and other entertainment and information products, more could be accomplished than with the election of an additional dozen senators of deep faith.

The *Los Angeles Times* is basically a nihilist and rudderless yet powerfully influential newspaper, as are the *Washington Post,* the *New York Times,* and a half-dozen other dailies. Even one of those papers in the hands of folks determined to help chart a course toward moral renewal could accomplish so much. No doubt the idea would be shocking to self-anointed guardians of the debased culture, but private efforts to steer a new course have an example in William Garrison's *The Liberator,* the newspaper that set itself a course that could be reached only with the abolition of slavery.

There are broader imperatives as well, one of which undergirds the next chapter. But a second defense to the temptation to give in and retreat is complete in itself: The gospel forbids our abandonment of the lost and the suffering.

In the spring of last year, I was asked to give the keynote address at an interfaith breakfast. One of my colleagues on the program was Denny Bilesci, the pastor of Coast Hills Community Church in Aliso Viejo, California—a vibrant and growing church. After my television series ran and after I had sent Denny a copy of the book, he called and asked me to participate in a couple of services specifically designed to reach spiritually restless "seekers." I agreed, and while listening from the audience heard him preach a sermon that drove home a gospel teaching that cannot be overemphasized.

Denny turned to the fifteenth chapter of Luke. It reads, in its entirety:

Now the tax collectors and sinners were all drawing near to hear him. And the Pharisees and the scribes murmured, saying, "This man receives sinners and eats with them."

So he told them this parable: "What man of you, having a hundred sheep, if he has lost one of them, does not leave the ninety-nine in the wilderness, and go after the one which is lost, until he finds it?

And when he has found it, he lays it on his shoulders, rejoicing.

And when he comes home, he calls together his friends and his neighbors, saying to them, 'Rejoice with me, for I have found my sheep which was lost.' Just so, I tell you, there will be more joy in heaven over one sinner who repents than over ninety-nine righteous persons who need no repentance.

"Or what woman, having ten silver coins, if she loses one coin, does not light a lamp and sweep the house and seek diligently until she finds it? And when she has found it, she calls together her friends and neighbors, saying, 'Rejoice with me, for I have found the coin which I had lost.' Just so, I tell you, there is joy before the angels of God over one sinner who repents."

And he said, "There was a man who had two sons; and the younger of them said to his father, 'Father, give me the share of property that falls to me.' And he divided his living between them. Not many days later, the younger son gathered all he had and took his journey into a far country, and there he squandered his property in loose living. And when he had spent everything, a great famine arose in that country, and he began to be in want. So he went and joined himself to one of the citizens of that country, who sent him into his fields to feed swine. And he would gladly have fed on the pods that the swine ate; and no one gave him anything.

But when he came to himself he said, 'How many of my father's hired servants have bread enough and to spare, but I perish here with hunger! I will arise and go to my father, and I will say to him, "Father, I have sinned against heaven and before you; I am no longer worthy to be called your son; treat me as one of your hired servants.'" And he arose and came to his father. But while he was yet at a distance, his father saw him and had compassion, and ran and embraced him and kissed him. And the son said to him, 'Father, I have sinned against heaven and before you; I am no longer worthy to be called your son.' But the father said to his servants, 'Bring quickly the best robe, and put it on him; and put a ring on his hand, and shoes on his feet; and bring the fatted calf and kill it, and let us eat and make merry; for this my son was dead, and is alive again; he was lost, and is found.' And they began to make merry.

Now his elder son was in the field; and as he came and drew near to the house, he heard music and dancing. And he called one of the servants and asked what this meant. And he said to him, 'Your brother has come, and your father has killed the fatted calf, because he has received him safe and sound.' But he was angry and refused to go in. His father came out and entreated him, but he answered his father, 'Lo, these many years I have served you, and I never disobeyed your command; yet you never gave me a kid, that I might make merry with my friends. But when this son of yours came, who has devoured your living with harlots, you killed for him the fatted calf!' And he said to him, 'Son, you are always with me, and all that is mine is yours. It was fitting to make merry and be glad, for this your brother was dead, and is alive; he was lost, and is found.'

The three parables are about the lost—a lost sheep, a lost coin, a lost son. And each owner—the shepherd, the woman, and the father—is desperate to regain what is lost, even to the extent of abandoning ninety-nine sheep, turning the house upside down and inside out, and watching night and day for the return of the prodigal.

As Denny was explaining this trio of parables, he slowed down, and then his voice cracked a bit. "The Father cares about the lost," he said in a halting voice. "He cares so deeply about the lost."

Again, I was reminded of the desperation of God to gather each and every person to Himself and of the infinite compassion He has for the lost and the hopeless. His sorrow for the victims of this culture—the debased *and* the debasers, the murdered *and* the shooters, the addicts *and* the dope dealers, the homeless *and* the greedy—is so vast that to glimpse even a small portion of that infinite sadness is to be immersed in deep despair.

God loves even the most evil individual—values him or her as much as He does the most righteous man or woman on the earth. They are all equal in His eyes. He will not abandon them in this lifetime. And thus neither can the church.

And that's the danger of the Parallel Culture—many hundreds of thousands, even millions, are streaming into and through the gates of faith, but how many are going out? It is comfortable on the inside. It is safe. It is even joyous. But believers cannot stay there. They must understand that the lost are to be found, and while God does not need anyone's effort, grace will certainly oblige a believer to understand the immensity of God's love even for the lost. And that understanding prompts our replication of His desperate search to reach even those most repellent of our neighbors.

28

Find the Good and Praise It

I heard former Education Secretary and Tennessee Governor Lamar Alexander give a great speech in the fall of 1994 and decided to investigate. On the strength of his book, *Six Months Off,* I sent his presidential campaign the maximum contribution allowed by law. The reasons are many, but I judged him to be the best man running for president. By that I mean he evidenced the clearest combination of good policies, electability, and commitment to godly service. Yes, he was, and I suspect remains, an ambitious man. And, yes, he articulated a bunch of political positions I agreed with. But mostly I could envision him speaking plainly and effectively to the American people about the need for moral renewal.

And, crucially, I believed he could do so without threatening our express commitment to an absolute ban on the establishment of religion. So deep is the fear of theocracy in some influential quarters—an irrational yet present fear—that great care must be taken to respect our constitutional traditions.

I was deeply persuaded by that first speech because Alexander invoked the motto (and I believe he said "epitaph") of his late friend, the African-American novelist Alex Haley, who wrote *Roots:*

Find the good and praise it.

Even if it is not on Haley's tombstone, even if I got the story wrong, the force of that simple directive is immense. It is, in fact, the largest weapon in the arsenal of American renewal and spiritual rebirth. If only the Christians in the United States embraced and practiced this, the results would be astonishing.

I cannot prove this to you, but you can prove it to yourself with a simple test of the maxim.

If your children have done well in any endeavor or made you proud by their simple obedience, seek them out and praise them.

If your spouse has done a day's work well, praise him or her.

If an educator or a public servant, an editor or a merchant has done good, write him or her and say so.

The encouragement of the good, the holding up of the honorable and the noble, is a far more powerful antidote than the condemnation, however necessary, of evil.

Ted Turner offends, but his CNN saved broadcast news. I salute it at every turn.

The *Weekly Standard* is the best magazine in America and deserves even wider readership. Subscribe today by calling 800-701-3883.

Max Lucado is a man of God possessed of a quiet yet awe-inspiring charisma. Read his books. Tell your friends. Ask your paper's editor to review these books.

Brett Butler's example in the face of serious illness is the best thing to happen in baseball in three years. His courage is an inspiration, as is his great talent. Drop a line to *Sports Illustrated* saying so.

The list is literally endless.

When Pastor Greg Laurie was my guest on my local PBS show, *Life & Times,* dozens of viewers who had never called the station before despite a nightly invitation to do so, did so; and even more sent letters praising the station for showing an evangelical preacher in his element and for letting him talk. This chorus of viewer appreciation made it easier to argue for more serious conversations about theology.

The public support for a television series such as *Touched by an Angel* and *Seventh Heaven* is a critical expression of the better instincts of the viewing public. How many lazy viewers will moan when they notice the show is gone if crippled by ratings. Sponsors of such shows need to hear support.

Instead of boycotts, Christians need to organize buy-outs of the products of companies that are willing to find the good and praise it and support it commercially.

The application of this simple principle is a stealth approach to the culture. Intellectuals will hesitate even to criticize it for the hokey, rube-like innocence it embodies because to take notice of the simple tactic is to be obliged to admit its effectiveness.

I speak once a week, on average, to a significant crowd. Often I am paid an astonishing amount of money to do so. Audiences thus expect a great deal. Almost inevitably I take pains to instruct them on this maxim—find the good and praise it—and it almost always sticks. It is the distillation of many books of ancient wisdom, and its simple force can disarm even cynical audiences. Why? Because everyone who has been praised remembers the occasion and cherishes it. "This is my beloved Son, with whom I am well pleased," said God the Father on the occasion of Jesus' baptism. We would do well to follow God's example.

This directive is especially applicable within churches where elbows can be sharp, indeed, and where pastoral staff members especially are typically on the receiving end of many suggestions and much grief but very little praise. I have noticed in some of the literature of Promise Keepers an express underscoring of the need to hold up and encourage pastors. Again, this new and novel movement appears to have redis-covered a simple Christian directive in advance of the church at large.

When I sent my contribution to Lamar Alexander, I included a note that suggested he name his then-underway campaign by the phrase that resonated with me. He didn't, and I'm glad he chose a different direction; because it left that marvelous phrase underused until this book was ready. Many thanks, Mr. Secretary.

I've saved the toughest part for the end.

Christians are compelled to believe that faith in Christ is the exclusive means of gaining salvation. This is a difficult thing to believe, because so many Christians know good and, indeed, holy, people who are not Christians. Aware of this "narrow gate" problem and uncomfortable with the prospect of having their friends condemned, they throw Scripture overboard. Even as wonderful a Christian pastor as Cecil Murray, whom God has endowed in extraordinary ways, found room in my interview with him to run around the implications of traditional Christian theology:

HUGH HEWITT: Let's stay in the Jesus segment of the religious garden, to use your phrase. Is He the Son of God?

CECIL MURRAY: For Christians, not only is Jesus the Son of God, but Christianity says Jesus is *the way.* Buddhism means the enlightened way. Islam means the way. Judaism, the way. Taoism, the way. Jesus Christ is the Son of God in the regard that if I see what God looks like, God would look like Jesus. And what is that? A love that goes all of the way out of the way to help somebody who has lost the way. God is love; Jesus is love. And it is sacrificial love . . . and dying for me. So that this carpenter is the very embodiment of the invisible, indivisible God. If I could see what God looks like, He would look like Jesus. Jesus is the Son of God. It took us three hundred years to come to that formula. We still haven't finalized it. To say that God is on Mars and He sends down His Son, His Heir, to earth, and then He goes back to Mars, and He's coming back again one of these days, and everybody who's got his soul washed is going to Mars with Him, that is so childish and so useless and so unintelligent.

HUGH HEWITT: Then what does it mean when He calls himself the Narrow Gate?

CECIL MURRAY: He's talking to people who are His followers. I am the way. I am the only way for you. But to force Him on others. . . . The roots of religion bring up many branches. And *religion* comes from the Latin word *religare*, that means "to tie, to bind." I have no right to offend my Buddhist brother or sister. I have no right to offend my Jewish brother or sister, my Islamic brother or sister, my Hindu brother or sister. There are many ways to the top of the mountain. Jesus says, "Follow Me. I am the way. I am the door." But is there only one door to the house of God? Is God that poor at home design that He would not have many doors facing many directions? There were twelve gates to Jerusalem. And there were many doors to the temple. So I do not want to lock anybody in. "Here is the way for me. May I explain it to you? Would you like it? Good. Let's go together."

Now, Hugh, I think our salvation is not being of one philosophy but being of one program. We covenant with Jewish Temple Isaiah. We covenant with several Korean temples. We covenant with Suni Muslims and the nation of Islam. We do programs. We are not going to have the same theology, thank God! We're not going to have the same philosophy, thank God! But there are four housing projects that need us. Let's work on that, and that will keep us from working on each other. What you call God is your business. What I call God is my business. All I know is we can do God's business far better by helping the needy than by trying to convert each other.

HUGH HEWITT: What happens to the person, in any of those religions, but specifically in the African Methodist Episcopal Church, when they die? What happens to that soul?

CECIL MURRAY: The Bible gives us several options. One is conditional immortality. The good folks go to heaven. The bad folks go to hell. Another is that you are extinguished. You die. You're dead. You're done. That's it. Hope you enjoyed it. Another is that everything is reclaimed. Several levels, you go to 'em. When you reach the seventh level, you get the beatific vision of heaven. I believe (and I'd quit the ministry this moment if I did not believe it) that the spirit of a human being is the most crucial, the most beautiful thing in the world. That spirit lives on. This tent is vacated. That essential life goes on to existence of another kind. We describe it in many euphoric terms and all. But we do know that there have been genuine scientists who've had out-of-body experiences. "I have stood and seen my corporeal tent, and here I am floating above it." So we can no longer laugh at that. The spirit is what America is rediscovering now. America is discovering that materialism is not enough. Me-too-ism is not enough. Cynicism, pessimism, is not enough. So that spirit, when the body dies, lives on. Now whether or not there's a burning hell and all, we'll see.

Pastor Roberta Hestenes did not bolt for the door when I posed the same question to her, but she too signaled her unease with the scriptural directive:

HUGH HEWITT: Whenever I have talked about religion with nonbelievers or disbelievers (and I draw a distinction between them), I run into the objection that the narrow gate is a put-off to people. The claim to exclusivity to eternal life or salvation, or whatever tradition calls it, is negative to many people. Is there a narrow gate? In your view, do you have to believe certain things to have eternal life?

ROBERTA HESTENES: Jesus used the phrase, "the narrow gate." It's not a phrase that someone made up. He talked about the broad road that leads to destruction and the narrow road that leads to salvation. And research polls show that it's more off-putting, in fact, to not know what you believe.

We live in a relativistic and highly tolerant age. But I'm grateful, for instance, for a doctor who told me that I had a tumor and then told me what to do about the tumor. It wasn't good news in the short run, but it made a cure possible. Because then I could act on the facts. And Christianity has bad news in it. It says to people, "Hey, it's possible to go the wrong way. It's possible to screw up your life. It's possible to make decisions that lead to destruction. It's possible to live in such a way that relationships around you are contaminated. It's possible to live so selfishly that you not only hurt yourself, but you make the world a worse place." That's bad news when I have to face that. But that turns into good news when I discover that God has provided a way to put the wrong right, that there is a cure.

HUGH HEWITT: Let me put the hard question: You're very ecumenical in your efforts outside of your presidency, even in World Vision. You've dialogued with a lot of different traditions. Do you believe people who are not Christian can be at complete peace in a way that a Christian would be after death?

ROBERTA HESTENES: Let me rephrase that question. After death, who knows? This side of death, of course. I meet sincere adherents of many traditions, and I don't think Christians have a monopoly on a certain kind of emotional experience. I think you can be a sincere, peaceful adherent believer.

HUGH HEWITT: But do Christians have a monopoly on salvation?

ROBERTA HESTENES: I think that what Scripture says is that Jesus says, "I am the way, the truth, and the life." I believe that. Yes, I believe that.

HUGH HEWITT: What does that mean for someone watching who isn't a Christian?

ROBERTA HESTENES: Well, it's a struggle to work it out, to be honest. And it's one of those areas where I have struggled a good bit.

In the Book of Romans, the apostle Paul talks about people who have never heard the Jewish law; and yet God had put a conscience within them, and they were a law unto themselves. And there's more than a suggestion in that Romans language that God is absolutely fair and does not hold people accountable for that which they do not know and are unable to respond to. However, Paul says in Romans, chapter 3, that "all have sinned and fall short of the glory of God." Then he says in chapter 6 that "the gift of God is eternal life in Jesus Christ our Lord." I have to leave it there. I do believe Jesus is the way.

Even when I posed the question to Chuck Colson, the response suggested how troubling the Scriptures are on this point. He, too, shifted into the mode of "it is what it is," a very different one from his otherwise earnest and inviting and enthused approach:

HUGH HEWITT: People are going to be mad at you, Chuck Colson. You're violating the great American principle of never claiming something to be absolutely true. You're claiming that Christianity is absolutely true.

CHARLES COLSON: That's right. People are saying that there are no absolutes except that there absolutely is no absolute. Christianity is an affront to the culture; it always has been.

HUGH HEWITT: That claim is also an affront to other religions, isn't it?

CHARLES COLSON: Yep. It's called the scandal of the cross, the scandal of the Star of David. It's the assertion that there is the God of Abraham, Isaac, and Jacob; there is the God of Jesus; there is one true God. That has always been an offense. And particularly so in American society today, when the ultimate virtue worshiped is tolerance. Anything goes. If it's true for you, that's fine; you do that. If it's true for me, I can do what I want. Which is a perfect prescription for moral chaos. That's exactly the reason people are searching for God. Our society is crumbling because we don't believe there are any absolutes. But there are.

HUGH HEWITT: Well, then, what is going to happen? What's your understanding of what's going to happen to the devout and holy Muslim, the devout and holy Buddhist, the devout and holy Hindu? They may be working alongside your ministry in the prisons, or they may be some of the people in prison who have been forgotten.

CHARLES COLSON: I can't judge that because I'm not God. All I know is what Jesus said: "No man comes to the Father but through Me." So I believe that the only way to God is through Jesus Christ.

Now, don't take offense at me. I'm quoting the Scripture of the Christ I know. And I know Him because He has come into my life and lives in me. I know Him because the historical evidence is absolutely overwhelming that He died on the cross and was raised again. So I believe His Word.

I fully respect the Muslim who believes something else. Although Muslims *do* believe in Jesus. They believe that instead of being bodily resurrected, He was somehow assumed into heaven. The Buddhist really does not believe in one God. But Jews, Muslims, and Christians all believe in one true God. The question is how to get to Him.

What all my guests were balancing was not truth versus doubt but the knowledge that a vast audience of nonbelievers was watching them explain these difficult texts. And even a slightly evangelical Christian knows that "narrow gate" exclusivity is a huge and powerful stumbling block to our contemporary culture. This is a culture that has enshrined tolerance, and there is in the claim of Christ's exclusivity an impossible-to-miss eternal intolerance.

The obvious misconceptions can be dealt with fairly rapidly. There is no Christian mandate to deal harshly with nonbelievers. In fact, the opposite is quite clearly ordered. And kindness and forgiveness, the Gospels suggest, are often going to be found outside the faith—recall the Good Samaritan. No, the Christian call is to live fully and in community with nonbelievers and to give to them even a greater measure of self than one gives to believers.

But Christ was clear in His words:

I am the way, and the truth, and the life; no one comes to the Father, but by me. (John 14:6)

Christ's earliest followers understood these words. Peter boldly asserted to a hostile Jerusalem that "There is salvation in no one else, for there is no other name under heaven given among men by which we must be saved" (Acts 4:12). The narrow-gate image is also expressly Christ's. "Enter by the narrow gate; for the gate is wide and the way is easy, that leads to destruction, and those who enter by it are many. For the gate is narrow and the way is hard, that leads to life, and those who find it are few" (Matthew 7:13–14).

It is, in my view, impossible to mistake the command Christ gives those who believe in Him. They are not to present Him as one among many options. He's not the greatest teacher in the world's history, as one nonbeliever told me in the course of the past year, a dodge so old that I thought it had been retired with "the cat's pajamas." No, Christ's instruction is direct, and the Christian must not deny it. Period.

Jesus established the narrow gate. He declared it. And we who believe in Him are obliged to believe He meant it and to tell our non-believing acquaintances *exactly* what He said.

I do pray that there is something not revealed to us that will operate after this life. God is all-merciful. But my job is simply to get it right. And Jesus understood how difficult this message was, so He kept it simple.

Christians cannot punt.

And there is a very good reason not to. The integrity of the gospel is deeply connected to its wholeness. It's not a menu where some of the teachings can be ordered and others abandoned. That practice forces its rapid unraveling and robs it of its full force.

That corrosive practice of customizing Christ according to our own wants and needs has zapped modern Christianity of a great deal of will and purpose. "A lot of Protestant theology doesn't stand firm anywhere," Dr. Nasr told me. "Every few years it changes positions on the basis of what happens to be fashionable at the time."

How can it be that a devout Muslim is more capable of succinctly naming some of the problems of Christianity than many Christians? The Embarrassed Believer has got to master the theology of the "narrow gate," because the secular world long ago diagnosed the discomfort that Christians have in asserting and defending the direction of Christ on this matter. Here is a challenge for pastors and lay leaders: Teach this part of the faith and teach it with thoroughness and passion. If Christians can feel comfortable in this area of their creed, they will certainly be equipped to defend the creed in its entirety.

"No One Would Make Up a Religion Like Christianity"

Through almost two hundred pages, I have tried to bait a trap. It is a good trap, but it is nevertheless a trap.

C. S. Lewis invented a devil and named him Screwtape. In the *Screwtape Letters* this devil gave advice to a colleague. Screwtape instructed the younger tempter, Wormwood, to keep his "patient"—the soul in peril of eternal damnation—firmly attentive to the immediate. "The trouble about argument," counseled Screwtape, "is that it moves the whole struggle onto the enemy's own ground." Screwtape expanded:

> By the every act of arguing, you awake the patient's reason; and once it is awake, who can foresee the result? Even if a particular train of thought can be twisted so as to end in our favour, you will find that you have been awakening the fatal habit of attending to universal issues and withdrawing his attention from the stream of immediate sense experiences. Your business is to fix his attention on the stream. Teach him to call it "real life" and don't let him ask what he means by real.

It is the task of modern people to attack the limits of their attention span. That means we must work—hard—at understanding God. This is a study that is not always pleasant. It's not a Tom Clancy novel. It's not *People* magazine. It is most assuredly not *Oprah*. Those things are fun, entertaining, and even occasionally informative. But not hard.

The study of God can be very, very hard.

But it is a complete reward.

The search for God in America took me to conversations with some of the country's better thinkers and speakers on theology. But it also took me to the library to find and excerpt writings by Americans on the subject of God. Because my first book on this subject was a survey, I included a great number of selections from atheists as well as selections from dozens of non-Christians.

And I kept up the search, even after round one was done. There is much, much more on the shelves than I was able to sample during the year leading up to the publication of *Searching for God in America.*

And of course there is the vast literature on God and His nature that has no American connection and was thus defined out of my first book. Even a morning in a fairly decent library impresses on the interested one the overwhelming amount of effort that human history records going into the enterprise of understanding God. And that, of course, is only the smallest slice of the total—it's the stuff that found its way into writing and has been preserved.

Earlier in this book I referred to a February 1993 *Washington Post* story on the "Gospel Grapevine." Here is what the *Post* staff writer had to say:

> The gospel lobby evolved with the explosion of satellite and cable television, hitting its national political peak in the presidential election of Ronald Reagan in 1980.
>
> Unlike other powerful interests, it does not lavish campaign funds on candidates for Congress nor does it entertain them. The strength of the fundamentalist leaders lies in their flocks. Corporations pay public relations firms millions of dollars to contrive the kind of grass-roots response that Falwell or Pat Robertson can galvanize in a televised sermon. Their followers are largely poor, uneducated and easy to command.

On February 2, 1993, the *Post* issued a correction: "An article yesterday characterized followers of television evangelists Jerry Falwell and Pat Robertson as 'largely poor, uneducated and easy to command.' There is no factual basis to that statement."

Note a few things. First, the original libel was not limited to followers of Jerry Falwell or Pat Robertson. In context, it is clearly applicable to followers of all "fundamentalist leaders." And it is not a stretch to smell the general anti-believer bias in the entire article. The "gospel grapevine" was defined to include the twelve hundred Christian radio stations and even such programs as *Focus on the Family.* The implication of "poor, uneducated and easy to command," is general, not specific.

That prejudice against believers has penetrated the culture. It is deep. It is thorough. Indeed, it is violent. And it is not content. Even in the face of systematic disparagement of belief, one of the nation's leading weeklies, the *New Republic,* actually ran a cover story in the fall of 1996 entitled: "The Last Taboo: Politicians Keep Saying We Should Inject More Religion into Our Public Life. But What We Really Need Is a Healthy Dose of Atheism." The central thesis of this piece? Well, it was the same, recycled anti-Christian rhetoric we saw in the *Post:*

> Religions, of course, have their own demanding intellectual traditions, as Jesuits and Talmudic scholars might attest. Smart people do believe in Gods and devote themselves to uncovering Their truths. But, in its less rigorous forms, religion is about as intellectually challenging as the average self-help book.

The author, Wendy Kaminer, "a Public Policy Fellow at Radcliffe College," continued:

> The marginal thinking encouraged by any belief in the supernatural, combined with the vilification of rationality and skepticism, is more conducive to conspiracy theories than it is productive debate. Conspiratorial thinking abounds during this period of spiritual and religious revivalism.

And there it is again! Those right-wing Christians and their conspiracy theories. If it's in the *New Republic, Harper's,* and the *Washington Post,* it must be true, right?

Another even more recent entrant in the lists of anti-Christian media sideswipes came in the aftermath of 1997's "Volunteer Summit" in Philadelphia. The *Los Angeles Times's* political writer, Robert Shogun, filed a report that included these three paragraphs:

> The harshest rhetoric about the conference came from the peripheries of the ideological spectrum.
>
> On the right, the Reverend Pat Robertson commended the goals of

the meeting but fretted during one of his "700 Club" television broadcasts that "what starts out as a noble initiative" can become a coercive effort on the government's part. He added: "And then you've got the Hitler youth corps, you know, where all the young frauleins have to run and put on their little uniforms and march to the Fuhrer."

On the left, "Workers World" published by the self-described "independent Marxist-Leninist" Workers World Party, called the conference a "multi-million dollar exercise in hypocrisy."

A few points need underscoring. First, Shogun put Robertson on the "peripher[y] of the ideological spectrum." That's a blatant lie, one that does not stand up to any reasonable critique. You may dislike his politics and criticize his theory, but Robertson is not on the "peripher[y] of the ideological spectrum."

Second, Shogun proved my own point by giving us a reference by which to measure Robertson. Shogun deftly equated the writers at "Workers World" to Robertson. The far left of "Workers World" does have a counterpart on the far right—groups just as small, just as splintered, and just as obviously removed from the country's politics. But any reader who knows politics knows that Robertson is well within the mainstream of America politics and the American political tradition, and that a writer who equates Robertson's stature with that of "Workers World" is either ignorant or biased.

Finally, note how Shogun's chronic anti-Christian bias drove him into a hilarious bind. So tempted was he by the "Hitler youth corps" quote—Shogun must believe that it makes Robertson sound loony—that he tried to use it to prove that Robertson is a fascist. Thus Shogun suggested that Robertson is a fascist and provided as his proof a Robertson quote condemning Hitler youth. Go figure.

There is no conspiracy among these papers and journals. There is, however, a parallel obtuseness. There is a fairly predictable antireligious bias that colors modern elite media and academia— but no conspiracy.

This prejudiced obtuseness is powerful but only if unanswered. And the answers are available, beginning with the sources I have referenced throughout this book and also with the facts of modern American life. The theological bedrock that strengthens believers in their belief was acknowledged even by Kaminer with her throwaway compliment to the Jesuits and Talmudic scholars (and what are the latter except Bible students?). More important, however, is the evidence of changed lives mounting up in church after church in the United States

Our culture is pulverizing youth—destroying their bodies and their souls. Our culture is savaging families, and its endless, ceaseless eroticism is attacking the dignity of women on a near-uninterrupted basis. The music is vile, and most of the films plumb evil's depths rather than goodness's heights.

Folks get chewed up by this accumulation of horrors.

Two subsets of our people should interest us in light of this maelstrom.

Who emerges unscathed and functioning?

Who is wounded but recovers?

In both instances I believe it is the believers. Here is why. If you have nonbeliever friends, photocopy for them this page and send it along with a note. Explain that whatever they think about Christianity, this small excerpt of the twelfth chapter of Paul's epistle to the Romans is as good a distillation of the Christian life as they will find:

> Let love be genuine; hate what is evil, hold fast to what is good; love one another with brotherly affection; outdo one another in showing honor. Never flag in zeal, be aglow with the Spirit, serve the Lord. Rejoice in your hope, be patient in tribulation, be constant in prayer. Contribute to the needs of the saints, practice hospitality.
>
> Bless those who persecute you; bless and do not curse them. Rejoice with those who rejoice, weep with those who weep. Live in harmony with one another; do not be haughty, but associate with the lowly; never be conceited. Repay no one evil for evil, but take thought for what is noble in the sight of all. If possible, so far as it depends upon you, live peaceably with all. Beloved, never avenge yourselves, but leave it to the wrath of God; for it is written, "Vengeance is mine, I will repay, says the Lord." No, "if your enemy is hungry, feed him; if he is thirsty, give him drink; for by so doing you will heap burning coals upon his head." Do not be overcome by evil, but overcome evil with good. (vv. 9–21)

When I read this passage and hundreds of others, I am reminded of what Chuck Colson said to me: "No one would make up a religion like

Christianity. It goes against every single one of our natural human instincts. Nobody's going to invent a religion that tells us to love our enemies, turn the other cheek, overcome evil with good. Nobody's going to do that. The gospel is a radical message that could only have come from God."

Nonbelievers thinking seriously about the big issues are stuck. They are on the flypaper—they are into the quicksand. Whether doubters are pushed far enough back to the beginning of time or far enough into the quietest part of their hearts, if they will pause long enough and genuinely ask, they will believe. "This is a mystery that you can't really convince people of unless they pray," Thomas Keating, the abbot in the mountains, told me. "It will become quite clear if one prays on a regular basis, because there God can speak to us in the silence of our heart and is not yet shut out by our thoughts and our pre-packaged values and presuppositions."

I want to close this book by borrowing from the close of another book. I am as far removed from the hard sciences as one can be. Once the SATs were safely behind me in 1974, I left physics and calculus and anything remotely related to them behind. I satisfied my undergraduate science requirements with the Sociology of Cancer and Natural Selection. And to this day, when called upon to interview scientists, especially the big guns like Edward Teller, I am at sea by page 3.

One of those "very smart" science guys is Dr. Robert Jastrow, director of the Mount Wilson Institute, which manages the Mount Wilson Observatory in California. Dr. Jastrow is the author of *God and the Astronomers,* a compelling account of the philosophical implications of the Big Bang theory. Jastrow concludes his book by sounding the sigh of the scientific community confronting the beginning of the universe:

> Now we would like to pursue that inquiry farther back in time, but the barrier to further progress seems insurmountable. It is not a matter of another year, another decade of work, another measurement, or another theory; at this moment it seems as though science will never be able to raise the curtain on the mystery of creation. For the scientist who has lived by his faith in the power of reason, the story ends like a bad dream. He has scaled the mountains of ignorance; he is about to conquer the

highest peak; as he pulls himself over the final rock, he is greeted by a band of theologians who have been sitting there for centuries.

It is perhaps unexciting to keep ending books the same way. But the obvious needs to be underscored again and again. I quote myself from my last book: "Search for God in America and you will find God in America. And then God will say 'Welcome. I am happy. And here's what you are going to do now.'"

Conclusion

Since the summer of 1996, when *Searching for God in America* aired, hardly a week has passed without some surprising effect arising from my having hosted a rather humble television series. I've received a number of invitations to talk to groups and conferences that are expressly Christian in their organization or purpose, and I am pleased to accept those that I can. But I'm even more encouraged by the number of the secular groups that have asked me to speak on the subject of spiritual seeking. In the early winter of 1997, for example, I was scheduled to give a talk to a bunch of homebuilders. When I'm not wandering around television studios or classrooms, I'm a pretty fair land-use lawyer who knows a few things about endangered species and wetlands.

When it came time to provide the logistical details of the speech, the fellow leaving the message on my voicemail haltingly mixed in the request that perhaps I could "cover the searching-for-God stuff" as well as the latest developments in the Fifth Amendment Takings case law.

Now, that's a tough choice!

Of course I did. I'm pleased and gratified to do so. My disclaimer is practiced now: "I'm not a pastor or a theologian. I'm just a broadcast journalist." And then it's into the breach.

What breach?

There is a vast and gaping hole in the middle of modern life. It's the old God-shaped hole in the soul. As Augustine said: "Oh, God, you formed me for yourself; and I have no rest until I rest in you." The modern world has rushed far away from God, and the compass was dropped along the way.

I'm one of those folks who is completely useless outdoors. My brother-in-law, sturdy retired United States Marine lieutenant colonel that he is, tried to educate me in the use of a compass one summer. I gave it a whirl . . . and stopped pretending to learn. "Lead on, George," was my answer. I wasn't lost, though, because I was with a fellow who wasn't lost.

Many, many people are lost because not only do they not know how to work the compass, neither does anyone else they know. And the sad part is they'd just as soon not be lost.

Add up the tens of millions of folks who are in that situation, and you get the culture we have: Deeply disturbed and horribly scarred and scared but restless and searching at the same time.

Believers need to start pointing and saying, "It's over there." They need to be firm, and they need to be heard. There should be an urgency in their call. They've got the compass, and they can use it. They've got to bring the lost along with them.

The single most important lesson I've learned from the past two years is that God called me to point the way to a few people, and He calls every single Christian to do the very same thing in a thousand different ways. It's not a unique job. It requires very little training. Literally everyone can do it.

And it is *not* an option. It's a command.

Still, believers hold back, embarrassed by their lack of deep learning, their stumbling explanations, or their fear of scorn. Every day millions of believers sit tight, waiting for their neighbors or the world to change, perhaps praying for a miracle but doing nothing. They are afraid of the risk.

The Appendix includes the book of Scripture named Ecclesiastes. It's a hard book, and many incorrectly believe that it leads a reader to despair. It actually should lead a reader to bold witness, because its narrative demolishes the idea of competing priorities. If the voice of Ecclesiastes is heard, believers recognize that nothing else matters, nothing else endures, except the relationship between the believer and God. What possible source of scorn could matter in comparison? What loss of status, power, influence, or money could count?

Put another way, Ecclesiastes reminds us that the cover stories in *Time* magazine, the Oscar speeches, and the State of the Union addresses are in the process of crumbling into dust before they can begin; so it is of no consequence whether the dominant opinion class sneers at or ignores expressions of belief. All of our pastimes, pursuits, careers, hobbies, hopes, and fears boil down to a chasing after wind. Once that central fact is grasped—really understood—the believer cannot be embarrassed.

Read Ecclesiastes. Then read the Gospels. And then act upon both.

ECCLESIASTES

OR THE PREACHER

1 The words of the Preacher, the son of David, king in Jerusalem.

2 "Vanity of vanities," says the
Preacher;
"Vanity of vanities, all is vanity."
3 What profit has a man from all his
labor
In which he toils under the sun?
4 One generation passes away, and
another generation comes;
But the earth abides forever.
5 The sun also rises, and the sun goes
down,
And hastens to the place where it
arose.
6 The wind goes toward the south,
And turns around to the north;
The wind whirls about continually,
And comes again on its circuit.
7 All the rivers run into the sea,
Yet the sea is not full;
To the place from which the rivers
come,
There they return again.
8 All things are full of labor;
Man cannot express it.
The eye is not satisfied with seeing,
Nor the ear filled with hearing.
9 That which has been is what will be,
That which is done is what will be
done,
And there is nothing new under the
sun.
10 Is there anything of which it may be
said,
"See, this is new"?
It has already been in ancient times
before us.
11 There is no remembrance of former
things,
Nor will there be any remembrance
of things that are to come
By those who will come after.

12 I, the Preacher, was king over Israel in Jerusalem. 13 And I set my heart to seek and search out by wisdom concerning all that is done under heaven; this burdensome task God has given to the sons of man, by which they may be exercised. 14 I have seen all the works that are done under the sun; and indeed, all is vanity and grasping for the wind.

15 What is crooked cannot be made
straight,
And what is lacking cannot be
numbered.

16 I communed with my heart, saying, "Look, I have attained greatness, and have gained more wisdom than all who were before me in Jerusalem. My heart has understood great wisdom and knowledge." 17 And I set my heart to know wisdom and to know madness and folly. I perceived that this also is grasping for the wind.

18 For in much wisdom is much grief,
And he who increases knowledge
increases sorrow.

2 I said in my heart, "Come now, I will test you with mirth; therefore enjoy pleasure"; but surely, this also was vanity. 2 I said of laughter—"Madness!"; and of mirth, "What does it accomplish?" 3 I searched in my heart how to gratify my flesh with wine, while guiding my heart with wisdom, and how to lay hold on folly, till I might see what was good for the sons of men to do under heaven all the days of their lives.

4 I made my works great, I built myself houses, and planted myself vineyards. 5 I made myself gardens and orchards, and I planted all kinds of fruit trees in them. 6 I made myself water pools from which to water the growing trees of the grove. 7 I acquired male and female servants, and had servants born in my house. Yes, I had greater possessions of herds and flocks

than all who were in Jerusalem before me. [8]I also gathered for myself silver and gold and the special treasures of kings and of the provinces. I acquired male and female singers, the delights of the sons of men, and musical instruments of all kinds.

[9] So I became great and excelled more than all who were before me in Jerusalem. Also my wisdom remained with me.

[10] Whatever my eyes desired I did not
    keep from them.
I did not withhold my heart from
    any pleasure,
For my heart rejoiced in all my
    labor;
And this was my reward from all my
    labor.
[11] Then I looked on all the works that
    my hands had done
And on the labor in which I had
    toiled;
And indeed all was vanity and
    grasping for the wind.
There was no profit under the sun.

[12] Then I turned myself to consider
    wisdom and madness and folly;
For what can the man do who suc-
    ceeds the king?—
Only what he has already done.
[13] Then I saw that wisdom excels folly
    As light excels darkness.
[14] The wise man's eyes are in his head,
But the fool walks in darkness.
Yet I myself perceived
That the same event happens to
    them all.
[15] So I said in my heart,
"As it happens to the fool,
It also happens to me,
And why was I then more wise?"
Then I said in my heart,
"This also is vanity."
[16] For there is no more remembrance
    of the wise than of the fool for-
    ever,
Since all that now is will be forgot-
    ten in the days to come.
And how does a wise man die?
As the fool!

[17] Therefore I hated life because the work that was done under the sun was distressing to me, for all is vanity and grasping for the wind.
[18] Then I hated all my labor in which I had toiled under the sun, because I must leave it to the man who will come after me. [19] And who knows whether he will be wise or a fool? Yet he will rule over all my labor in which I toiled and in which I have shown myself wise under the sun. This also is vanity. [20] Therefore I turned my heart and despaired of all the labor in which I had toiled under the sun. [21] For there is a man whose labor is with wisdom, knowledge, and skill; yet he must leave his heritage to a man who has not labored for it. This also is vanity and a great evil. [22] For what has man for all his labor, and for the striving of his heart with which he has toiled under the sun? [23] For all his days are sorrowful, and his work burdensome; even in the night his heart takes no rest. This also is vanity.

[24] Nothing is better for a man than that he should eat and drink, and that his soul should enjoy good in his labor. This also, I saw, was from the hand of God. [25] For who can eat, or who can have enjoyment, more than I? [26] For God gives wisdom and knowledge and joy to a man who is good in His sight; but to the sinner He gives the work of gathering and collecting, that he may give to him who is good before God. This also is vanity and grasping for the wind.

3 To everything there is a season,
    A time for every purpose under
        heaven:
[2] A time to be born,
    And a time to die;
A time to plant,
    And a time to pluck what is
        planted;
[3] A time to kill,
    And a time to heal;
A time to break down,
    And a time to build up;
[4] A time to weep,
    And a time to laugh;
A time to mourn,
    And a time to dance;
[5] A time to cast away stones,
    And a time to gather stones;
A time to embrace,
    And a time to refrain from
        embracing;
[6] A time to gain,
    And a time to lose;
A time to keep,
    And a time to throw away;
[7] A time to tear,
    And a time to sew;

A time to keep silence,
And a time to speak;
8 A time to love,
And a time to hate;
A time of war,
And a time of peace.

9 What profit has the worker from that in which he labors? 10I have seen the God-given task with which the sons of men are to be occupied. 11He has made everything beautiful in its time. Also He has put eternity in their hearts, except that no one can find out the work that God does from beginning to end. 12 I know that nothing is better for them than to rejoice, and to do good in their lives, 13and also that every man should eat and drink and enjoy the good of all his labor—it is the gift of God.

14 I know that whatever God does,
It shall be forever.
Nothing can be added to it,
And nothing taken from it.
God does it, that men should fear
before Him.
15 That which is has already been,
And what is to be has already been;
And God requires an account of
what is past.

16 Moreover I saw under the sun:

In the place of judgment,
Wickedness was there;
And in the place of righteousness,
Iniquity was there.

17 I said in my heart,

"God shall judge the righteous and
the wicked,
For there is a time there for every
purpose and for every work."

18 I said in my heart, "Concerning the condition of the sons of men, God tests them, that they may see that they themselves are like animals." 19For what happens to the sons of men also happens to animals; one thing befalls them: as one dies, so dies the other. Surely, they all have one breath; man has no advantage over animals, for all is vanity. 20All go to one place: all are from the dust, and all return to dust. 21Who knows the spirit of the sons of men, which goes upward, and the spirit of the animal, which goes down to the earth? 22So I perceived that nothing is better than that a man should rejoice in his own works, for that is his heritage. For who can bring him to see what will happen after him?

4 Then I returned and considered all the oppression that is done under the sun:

And look! The tears of the
oppressed,
But they have no comforter—
On the side of their oppressors there
is power,
But they have no comforter.
2 Therefore I praised the dead who
were already dead,
More than the living who are still
alive.
3 Yet, better than both is he who has
never existed,
Who has not seen the evil work that
is done under the sun.

4 Again, I saw that for all toil and every skillful work a man is envied by his neighbor. This also is vanity and grasping for the wind.

5 The fool folds his hands
And consumes his own flesh.
6 Better a handful with quietness
Than both hands full, together with
toil and grasping for the wind.

7 Then I returned, and I saw vanity under the sun:

8 There is one alone, without com-
panion:
He has neither son nor brother.
Yet there is no end to all his labors,
Nor is his eye satisfied with riches.
But he never asks,
"For whom do I toil and deprive
myself of good?"
This also is vanity and a grave mis-
fortune.

9 Two are better than one,
Because they have a good reward for
their labor.
10 For if they fall, one will lift up his
companion.
But woe to him who is alone when
he falls,
For he has no one to help him up.

¹¹Again, if two lie down together, they
will keep warm;
But how can one be warm alone?
¹²Though one may be overpowered by
another, two can withstand him.
And a threefold cord is not quickly
broken.

¹³Better a poor and wise youth
Than an old and foolish king who
will be admonished no more.
¹⁴For he comes out of prison to be
king,
Although he was born poor in his
kingdom.
¹⁵I saw all the living who walk under
the sun;
They were with the second youth
who stands in his place.
¹⁶There was no end of all the people
over whom he was made king;
Yet those who come afterward will
not rejoice in him.
Surely this also is vanity and grasping for the wind.

5 Walk prudently when you go to the
house of God; and draw near to hear
rather than to give the sacrifice of fools,
for they do not know that they do evil.

²Do not be rash with your mouth,
And let not your heart utter anything
hastily before God.
For God is in heaven, and you on
earth;
Therefore let your words be few.
³For a dream comes through much
activity,
And a fool's voice is known by his
many words.

⁴When you make a vow to God, do not
delay to pay it;
For He has no pleasure in fools.
Pay what you have vowed—
⁵Better not to vow than to vow and
not pay.

⁶Do not let your mouth cause your flesh
to sin, nor say before the messenger of
God that it was an error. Why should
God be angry at your excuse and
destroy the work of your hands? ⁷For
in the multitude of dreams and many
words there is also vanity. But fear
God.
⁸If you see the oppression of the poor,
and the violent perversion of justice and
righteousness in a province, do not marvel
at the matter; for high official watches
over high official, and higher officials are
over them.
⁹Moreover the profit of the land is for
all; even the king is served from the field.

¹⁰He who loves silver will not be satis-
fied with silver;
Nor he who loves abundance, with
increase.
This also is vanity.
¹¹When goods increase,
They increase who eat them;
So what profit have the owners
Except to see them with their eyes?
¹²The sleep of a laboring man is sweet,
Whether he eats little or much;
But the abundance of the rich will
not permit him to sleep.

¹³There is a severe evil which I have
seen under the sun:
Riches kept for their owner to his
hurt.
¹⁴But those riches perish through misfortune;
When he begets a son, there is nothing in his hand.
¹⁵As he came from his mother's womb,
naked shall he return,
To go as he came;
And he shall take nothing from his
labor
Which he may carry away in his
hand.
¹⁶And this also is a severe evil—
Just exactly as he came, so shall
he go.
And what profit has he who has
labored for the wind?
¹⁷All his days he also eats in darkness,
And he has much sorrow and sick-
ness and anger.

¹⁸Here is what I have seen: It is good
and fitting for one to eat and drink, and to
enjoy the good of all his labor in which he
toils under the sun all the days of his life
which God gives him; for it is his heritage.
¹⁹As for every man to whom God has
given riches and wealth, and given him
power to eat of it, to receive his heritage
and rejoice in his labor—this is the gift of
God. ²⁰For he will not dwell unduly on
the days of his life, because God keeps him
busy with the joy of his heart.

6 There is an evil which I have seen under the sun, and it is common among men: ²A man to whom God has given riches and wealth and honor, so that he lacks nothing for himself of all he desires; yet God does not give him power to eat of it, but a foreigner consumes it. This is vanity, and it is an evil affliction. ³If a man begets a hundred children and lives many years, so that the days of his years are many, but his soul is not satisfied with goodness, or indeed he has no burial, I say that a stillborn child is better than he— ⁴for it comes in vanity and departs in darkness, and its name is covered with darkness. ⁵Though it has not seen the sun or known anything, this has more rest than that man, ⁶even if he lives a thousand years twice—but has not seen goodness. Do not all go to one place?

⁷ All the labor of man is for his
    mouth,
  And yet the soul is not satisfied.
⁸ For what more has the wise man
    than the fool?
  What does the poor man have,
  Who knows how to walk before the
    living?
⁹ Better is the sight of the eyes than
    the wandering of desire.
  This also is vanity and grasping for
    the wind.

¹⁰ Whatever one is, he has been named
    already,
  For it is known that he is man;
  And he cannot contend with Him
    who is mightier than he.
¹¹ Since there are many things that
    increase vanity,
  How is man the better?

¹² For who knows what is good for man in life, all the days of his vain life which he passes like a shadow? Who can tell a man what will happen after him under the sun?

7 A good name is better than precious
    ointment,
  And the day of death than the day of
    one's birth;
² Better to go to the house of mourn-
    ing
  Than to go to the house of feasting,
  For that is the end of all men;
  And the living will take it to heart.

³ Sorrow is better than laughter,
  For by a sad countenance the heart
    is made better.
⁴ The heart of the wise is in the house
    of mourning,
  But the heart of fools is in the house
    of mirth.

⁵ It is better to hear the rebuke of the
    wise
  Than for a man to hear the song of
    fools.
⁶ For like the crackling of thorns
    under a pot,
  So is the laughter of the fool.
  This also is vanity.
⁷ Surely oppression destroys a wise
    man's reason,
  And a bribe debases the heart.

⁸ The end of a thing is better than its
    beginning;
  The patient in spirit is better than
    the proud in spirit.
⁹ Do not hasten in your spirit to be
    angry,
  For anger rests in the bosom of fools.
¹⁰ Do not say,
  "Why were the former days better
    than these?"
  For you do not inquire wisely con-
    cerning this.

¹¹ Wisdom is good with an inheri-
    tance,
  And profitable to those who see the
    sun.
¹² For wisdom is a defense as money is
    a defense,
  But the excellence of knowledge is
    that wisdom gives life to those
    who have it.

¹³ Consider the work of God;
  For who can make straight what He
    has made crooked?
¹⁴ In the day of prosperity be joyful,
  But in the day of adversity consider:
  Surely God has appointed the one as
    well as the other,
  So that man can find out nothing
    that will come after him.

¹⁵ I have seen everything in my days of
vanity:

  There is a just man who perishes in
    his righteousness,

And there is a wicked man who pro-
longs life in his wickedness.

16 Do not be overly righteous,
Nor be overly wise:
Why should you destroy yourself?
17 Do not be overly wicked,
Nor be foolish:
Why should you die before your
time?
18 It is good that you grasp this,
And also not remove your hand
from the other;
For he who fears God will escape
them all.

19 Wisdom strengthens the wise
More than ten rulers of the city.

20 For there is not a just man on earth
who does good
And does not sin.

21 Also do not take to heart everything
people say,
Lest you hear your servant cursing
you.
22 For many times, also, your own
heart has known
That even you have cursed others.

23 All this I have proved by wisdom.
I said, "I will be wise";
But it was far from me.
24 As for that which is far off and
exceedingly deep,
Who can find it out?
25 I applied my heart to know,
To search and seek out wisdom and
the reason of things,
To know the wickedness of folly,
Even of foolishness and madness.
26 And I find more bitter than death
The woman whose heart is snares
and nets,
Whose hands are fetters.
He who pleases God shall escape
from her,
But the sinner shall be trapped by
her.
27 "Here is what I have found," says the
Preacher,
"Adding one thing to the other to
find out the reason,
28 Which my soul still seeks but I cannot find:
One man among a thousand I have
found,

But a woman among all these I have
not found.
29 Truly, this only I have found:
That God made man upright,
But they have sought out many
schemes."

8 Who is like a wise man?
And who knows the interpretation
of a thing?
A man's wisdom makes his face
shine,
And the sternness of his face is
changed.

2 I say, "Keep the king's commandment for the sake of your oath to God.
3 "Do not be hasty to go from his presence.
Do not take your stand for an evil thing,
for he does whatever pleases him."

4 Where the word of a king is, there is
power;
And who may say to him, "What are
you doing?"
5 He who keeps his command will
experience nothing harmful;
And a wise man's heart discerns
both time and judgment,
6 Because for every matter there is a
time and judgment,
Though the misery of man increases
greatly.
7 For he does not know what will
happen;
So who can tell him when it will
occur?
8 No one has power over the spirit to
retain the spirit,
And no one has power in the day of
death.
There is no release from that war,
And wickedness will not deliver
those who are given to it.

9 All this I have seen, and applied my
heart to every work that is done under the
sun: There is a time in which one man
rules over another to his own hurt.

10 Then I saw the wicked buried, who
had come and gone from the place of holiness, and they were forgotten in the city
where they had so done. This also is vanity. 11 Because the sentence against an evil
work is not executed speedily, therefore
the heart of the sons of men is fully set in
them to do evil. 12 Though a sinner does
evil a hundred times, and his days are pro-

longed, yet I surely know that it will be well with those who fear God, who fear before Him. ¹³But it will not be well with the wicked; nor will he prolong his days, which are as a shadow, because he does not fear before God.

¹⁴ There is a vanity which occurs on earth, that there are just men to whom it happens according to the work of the wicked; again, there are wicked men to whom it happens according to the work of the righteous. I said that this also is vanity.

¹⁵So I commended enjoyment, because a man has nothing better under the sun than to eat, drink, and be merry; for this will remain with him in his labor all the days of his life which God gives him under the sun.

¹⁶ When I applied my heart to know wisdom and to see the business that is done on earth, even though one sees no sleep day or night, ¹⁷then I saw all the work of God, that a man cannot find out the work that is done under the sun. For though a man labors to discover it, yet he will not find it; moreover, though a wise man attempts to know it, he will not be able to find it.

9For I considered all this in my heart, so that I could declare it all: that the righteous and the wise and their works are in the hand of God. People know neither love nor hatred by anything they see before them. ²All things come alike to all:

One event happens to the righteous and the wicked;
To the good, the clean, and the unclean;
To him who sacrifices and him who does not sacrifice.
As is the good, so is the sinner;
He who takes an oath as he who fears an oath.

³ This is an evil in all that is done under the sun: that one thing happens to all. Truly the hearts of the sons of men are full of evil; madness is in their hearts while they live, and after that they go to the dead. ⁴But for him who is joined to all the living there is hope, for a living dog is better than a dead lion.

⁵ For the living know that they will die;

But the dead know nothing,
And they have no more reward,
For the memory of them is forgotten.
⁶ Also their love, their hatred, and their envy have now perished;
Nevermore will they have a share
In anything done under the sun.

⁷ Go, eat your bread with joy,
And drink your wine with a merry heart;
For God has already accepted your works.
⁸ Let your garments always be white,
And let your head lack no oil.

⁹ Live joyfully with the wife whom you love all the days of your vain life which He has given you under the sun, all your days of vanity; for that is your portion in life, and in the labor which you perform under the sun. ¹⁰Whatever your hand finds to do, do it with your might; for there is no work or device or knowledge or wisdom in the grave where you are going.

¹¹I returned and saw under the sun that—

The race is not to the swift,
Nor the battle to the strong,
Nor bread to the wise,
Nor riches to men of understanding,
Nor favor to men of skill;
But time and chance happen to them all.
¹² For man also does not know his time:
Like fish taken in a cruel net,
Like birds caught in a snare,
So the sons of men are snared in an evil time,
When it falls suddenly upon them.

¹³ This wisdom I have also seen under the sun, and it seemed great to me: ¹⁴There was a little city with few men in it; and a great king came against it, besieged it, and built great snares around it. ¹⁵Now there was found in it a poor wise man, and he by his wisdom delivered the city. Yet no one remembered that same poor man.

¹⁶Then I said:

"Wisdom is better than strength.
Nevertheless the poor man's wisdom is despised,

And his words are not heard.
17 Words of the wise, spoken quietly,
    should be heard
Rather than the shout of a ruler of
    fools.
18 Wisdom is better than weapons of
    war;
But one sinner destroys much good."

10 Dead flies putrefy the perfumer's
    ointment,
And cause it to give off a foul odor;
So does a little folly to one respected
    for wisdom and honor.
2 A wise man's heart is at his right
    hand,
But a fool's heart at his left.
3 Even when a fool walks along the
    way,
He lacks wisdom,
And he shows everyone that he is a
    fool.
4 If the spirit of the ruler rises against
    you,
Do not leave your post;
For conciliation pacifies great
    offenses.

5 There is an evil I have seen under
    the sun,
As an error proceeding from the
    ruler:
6 Folly is set in great dignity,
While the rich sit in a lowly place.
7 I have seen servants on horses,
While princes walk on the ground
    like servants.

8 He who digs a pit will fall into it,
And whoever breaks through a wall
    will be bitten by a serpent.
9 He who quarries stones may be hurt
    by them,
And he who splits wood may be
    endangered by it.
10 If the ax is dull,
And one does not sharpen the edge,
Then he must use more strength;
But wisdom brings success.

11 A serpent may bite when it is not
    charmed;
The babbler is no different.
12 The words of a wise man's mouth are
    gracious,
But the lips of a fool shall swallow
    him up;

13 The words of his mouth begin with
    foolishness,
And the end of his talk is raving
    madness.
14 A fool also multiplies words.
No man knows what is to be;
Who can tell him what will be after
    him?
15 The labor of fools wearies them,
For they do not even know how to
    go to the city!

16 Woe to you, O land, when your king
    is a child,
And your princes feast in the morn-
    ing!
17 Blessed are you, O land, when your
    king is the son of nobles,
And your princes feast at the proper
    time—
For strength and not for drunken-
    ness!
18 Because of laziness the building
    decays,
And through idleness of hands the
    house leaks.
19 A feast is made for laughter,
And wine makes merry;
But money answers everything.
20 Do not curse the king, even in your
    thought;
Do not curse the rich, even in your
    bedroom;
For a bird of the air may carry your
    voice,
And a bird in flight may tell the
    matter.

11 Cast your bread upon the waters,
    For you will find it after many
    days.
2 Give a serving to seven, and also to
    eight,
For you do not know what evil will
    be on the earth.

3 If the clouds are full of rain,
They empty themselves upon the
    earth;
And if a tree falls to the south or the
    north,
In the place where the tree falls,
    there it shall lie.
4 He who observes the wind will not
    sow,
And he who regards the clouds will
    not reap.

5 As you do not know what is the way
   of the wind,
Or how the bones grow in the
   womb of her who is with child,
So you do not know the works of
   God who makes everything.
6 In the morning sow your seed,
And in the evening do not with-
   hold your hand;
For you do not know which will
   prosper,
Either this or that,
Or whether both alike will be good.

7 Truly the light is sweet,
And it is pleasant for the eyes to
   behold the sun;
8 But if a man lives many years
And rejoices in them all,
Yet let him remember the days of
   darkness,
For they will be many.
All that is coming is vanity.

9 Rejoice, O young man, in your
   youth,
And let your heart cheer you in the
   days of your youth;
Walk in the ways of your heart,
And in the sight of your eyes;
But know that for all these
God will bring you into judgment.
10 Therefore remove sorrow from your
   heart,
And put away evil from your flesh,
For childhood and youth are vanity.

12 Remember now your Creator in
   the days of your youth,
Before the difficult days come,
And the years draw near when you
   say,
"I have no pleasure in them":
2 While the sun and the light,
The moon and the stars,
Are not darkened,
And the clouds do not return after
   the rain;
3 In the day when the keepers of the
   house tremble,
And the strong men bow down;
When the grinders cease because
   they are few,
And those that look through the
   windows grow dim;
4 When the doors are shut in the
   streets,

And the sound of grinding is low;
When one rises up at the sound of a
   bird,
And all the daughters of music are
   brought low;
5 Also they are afraid of height,
And of terrors in the way;
When the almond tree blossoms,
The grasshopper is a burden,
And desire fails.
For man goes to his eternal home,
And the mourners go about the
   streets.

6 Remember your Creator before the
   silver cord is loosed,
Or the golden bowl is broken,
Or the pitcher shattered at the foun-
   tain,
Or the wheel broken at the well.
7 Then the dust will return to the
   earth as it was,
And the spirit will return to God
   who gave it.
8 "Vanity of vanities," says the
   Preacher,
"All is vanity."

9 And moreover, because the Preacher
was wise, he still taught the people
knowledge; yes, he pondered and sought
out and set in order many proverbs. 10The
Preacher sought to find acceptable words;
and what was written was upright—words
of truth. 11 The words of the wise are like
goads, and the words of scholars are like
well-driven nails, given by one Shepherd.
12And further, my son, be admonished by
these. Of making many books there is no
end, and much study is wearisome to the
flesh.
13 Let us hear the conclusion of the
   whole matter:

   Fear God and keep His command-
      ments,
   For this is man's all.
14 For God will bring every work into
      judgment,
   Including every secret thing,
   Whether good or evil.

Acknowledgments

Once again, Amy Schroeder has been a research assistant of great ability and zeal. She finds what others only dream of finding. Curtis Yates took up those areas when Amy moved east and quickly mastered a position made harder to fill because it had been filled by a great friend as well as researcher. I thank them both.

Once again, Lynne Chapman prepared the manuscript with great skill and care.

Once again, Snow Philip scoured the text for the errors that seem to creep into every manuscript. Sue Ann Jones provided an edit as well that helped keep the book free of distracting errors.

My church has encouraged small-group fellowship for many years. My group consists of Richard Bryant, Bill Lobdell, Emmett Raitt, Mike Regele, and Mark Roberts. They are great and good friends to me and to this book. Mary Bryant, Greer Lobdell, Michelle Raitt, Debbie Regele, and Linda Roberts are the other halves of these great friends. Thanks to them as well.

Dean Dunn-Rankin, Charlie Exon, Bill Halle, Andrew Hartzell, Jack Hudson, Mark McGuire, Steve Odell, Dennis O'Neil, Jay Palchikoff, Paul Rowe, Bill Twomey, and John Yeager practice law with me. They cover for me when I'm writing, and they cheerfully watch the fax machine collapse under the weight of incoming and outgoing missives. All of them have been uniformly gracious, except Yeager on Mondays following a Packer loss.

Sealy and Susan Yates and Tom Thompson are a team of advisers without equal or near equal.

Joey Paul and Jana Muntsinger and all the folks at Word are working to heal a culture. Their ministry is succeeding because they pursue it with great zeal and yet with great kindness.

During the final edits on this book, Kip Jordon died. Kip was the longtime and much-loved leader at Word. He launched my first book and ordered up this one. His enthusiasm and love for God are examples of bold belief of the sort the rest of us can only hope to approach.

Martin Burns directed *Searching for God in America.* I'll be thanking him for as long as I write books with acknowledgments.

Larry Arnn is a teacher of incredible ability. He keeps pointing, and I keep finding. I thank him.

Betsy, Diana, William, and James make my life a great joy, which I hope is reflected in my writing.

Hugh Hewitt is the co-host of Los Angeles PBS affiliate KCET's nightly news show *Life & Times Tonight*. He is the author of two previous books, the winner of two Emmys, recipient of the 1997 Gold Medallion Book Award and the 1996 Wilbur Award from the Religious Public Relations Council. He is an honors graduate of Harvard College and the University of Michigan Law School. He served six years in the Reagan Administration in a variety of posts including Assistant Counsel in the White House. He is presently a law professor at Chapman University Law School in Orange, California.

Hugh Hewitt is available for a limited number of speaking engagements and is represented through Sealy M. Yates. For details, please call Susan Yates at 714-285-9540.